Burial Customs in Ancient Egypt

DUCKWORTH EGYPTOLOGY

Burial Customs in Ancient Egypt:
Life in Death for Rich and Poor

Wolfram Grajetzki

Duckworth

First published in 2003 by
Gerald Duckworth & Co. Ltd.
61 Frith Street, London W1D 3JL
Tel: 020 7434 4242
Fax: 020 7434 4420
inquiries@duckworth-publishers.co.uk
www.ducknet.co.uk

A catalogue record for this book is available
from the British Library

ISBN 0 7156 3217 5

Printed and bound in Great Britain by
Biddles Ltd, *www.biddles.co.uk*

Contents

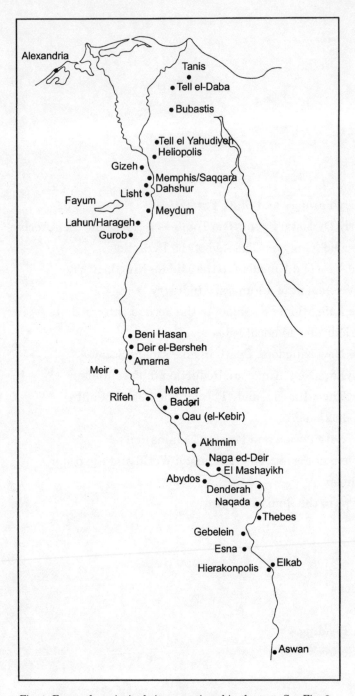

Fig. 1. Egypt: the principal sites mentioned in the text. See Fig. 2 for a detailed map of the Memphis-Fayum area.

Preface

The energy devoted by the ancient Egyptians to their tombs is legendary. The pyramids of Gizeh and the tomb of Tutankhamun are merely the two most spectacular examples. No previous book has sought to collect all the material from the tens of thousands of tombs excavated in Egypt to give a broad picture of what was placed in these tombs at different times and throughout society. This is surprising, though, to compensate, there are many books concentrating on mummies or on particular objects, such as coffins or amulets. There are also a few studies that investigate the rules about what went into tombs in particular periods. However, in general amazingly little attention has been paid to the burial equipment as a unit – that is, all the objects placed in an 'average' tomb at a given time.

This book was not easy to write, primarily because the recording and publication of finds has varied so much. There are many well-published tombs of the Old Kingdom, the period that has appealed most to those Egyptologists interested in archaeology as opposed to art and language. By contrast, later tombs and burials are often very badly published with inadequate descriptions; most often, sadly, they are not published at all. For these later periods, the focus of attention is too rarely the archaeological context. Instead, typologies have been more important for research, which has tended to concentrate on single objects, such as funerary papyri, coffins or pottery.

In writing this book, I have aimed not only to cover all periods as impartially as possible, but also, and equally importantly, to remove some widespread and unwarranted assumptions. The first of these concerns the archaeological record: many people still believe that there are only very few undisturbed tombs. This is simply not true. The number of unplundered burials – even for elite officials – of all periods is much higher than one might expect. Of course there are only a few examples overflowing with treasure, such as the tomb of Tutankhamun or the burials of the kings at Tanis. However, there are many well-preserved tombs with few or no gold objects which have not attracted so much attention. These are key sources for reconstructing burial customs and Egyptian culture as a whole.

A second unwarranted assumption is that we do not have the burials of the common farmers or poor people. Many Egyptologists still believe that a burial is automatically a sign of the higher status of the deceased. According to such opinion, the 'poor' were simply placed in the desert sand without any burial objects.[1] This is not the case. In the area of one provincial town, Qau, more than seven thousand tombs have been excavated, most of which must belong to farmers living in small villages along the desert edge of the region. Similar cemeteries have been found, excavated and published from other parts of the country: Bubastis, Gurob, Naga ed-Deir, Saqqara, Sedment. Admittedly, a distinction has to be made between 'poor (= not rich)' and 'poor (= destitute)'. We know almost nothing about the social structure in villages or towns, but this distinction can be assumed for ancient Egypt from parallels in other comparable societies. On the one hand there will have been the poorest people, such as beggars – outcasts from their society, with no property – who probably really have not left much trace in the archaeological record. On the other hand, there must have been large numbers of farmers with a small income, just enough to survive, and some property. These people were certainly buried with at least some expense. They had a family and work, and so were part of a supporting social structure. Their relatives must have spent some time digging tombs and equipping their beloved family members with at least some funerary objects, even if only a few pots or beads, if that was the custom of the day.

Population estimates for remote antiquity are extremely vague, but there is a general consensus that around a million people were living in Egypt by the time of the Old Kingdom. With four or five generations a century, this would mean that several hundred million people died and were buried in pharaonic Egypt. Each burial had its own character; even though there are points in common, no two burials are identical in layout and content. The following study can therefore only give an outline, describing the most typical items placed in tombs. The choice of burials described is very subjective. I have concentrated on what was 'normal' in each period, rather than what is best preserved or most colourful. Even specialised researchers often focus too heavily on some well-preserved monuments, which are sometimes not at all typical of their time. The list of further reading at the end of the book points the reader to sources of more detail on particular subjects.

I would like to thank Nicholas Reeves, Deborah Blake and Ray Davies from Duckworth for all their assistance in publishing this book. I am also grateful to Stephen Quirke for reading my English and many discussions on the subject. I would like to thank Christian Loeben for providing me with some of the more inaccessible literature on coffins, Rita Freed for the opportunity to study the Reisner records in Boston, and Eberhard Holzhäuer, director of DASS (database of ancient Egyptian coffins and sarcophagi) for the years I worked for his project, offering me extensive contact with funerary culture in Ancient Egypt. Finally, I wish to acknowledge my indebtedness to Stefan Seidlmayer, both for his publications and for a colloquium he organised at the Freie Universität Berlin in 1990. The responsibility for the contents of this book is, of course, my own.

W.G.

1. Early Farmers and State Formation

The earliest known farming communities in Egypt are from the Fayum area, where settlements dating to around 5000 BC have been excavated. Although the excavators of these sites tried hard to find cemeteries, or at least some tombs, so far no burial places of these early farmers have been located. At about the same time in Lower Egypt, the Delta settlement of Merimde flourished. A Neolithic (stone age agricultural) society, the Merimde people produced simple pottery including clay figurines, cultivated wheat and kept domesticated cattle and other animals. Altogether the settlement was inhabited for about a thousand years. The inhabitants buried their people within the settlement area. They did not create special cemeteries; graves were found by the excavators just next to houses, or sometimes even inside them. Admittedly the archaeological context is not entirely clear. Were the dead really buried inside or under habitations, or in buildings that were empty and uninhabited by the time of the burial? The dead were placed in shallow holes in a contracted position. There are almost no objects in these tombs and there seems to be no rule about the orientation of the body. Unlike the later Egyptians, the Merimde people seem not to be very concerned about their dead.[1]

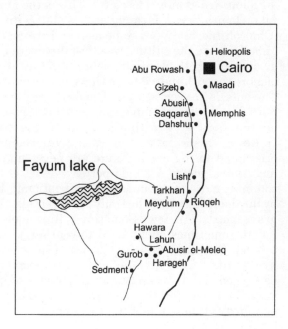

Fig. 2.
The Memphis-Fayum area.

Another Neolithic people in Lower Egypt are known as the Omari culture, which flourished around 4600-4400 BC. It is known from only a few sites, and is contemporary with the later phases of the Merimde culture. Cattle, pigs

Fig. 3. Examples of vessels found in tombs of the Omari culture.

and goats had been domesticated here, and several kinds of wheat were cultivated, though metal was not yet known. A settlement has been excavated near Helwan, today a suburb south of Cairo. The people of the Omari culture lived in small houses partly cut into the ground and buried their dead partly inside their settlements in shallow pits. The bodies were placed lying on their left side with the head to the south in a contracted position, and with the hands in front of the face. The dead were quite often laid in mats; there is no sign of any wrappings or other textiles. This is not simply a question of preservation, as some textiles have survived in the settlement itself. Evidently the deceased were placed naked in their tombs. One pot as grave good was normal, with no personal adornments – these are very typical of many periods and cultures. The pots were often found filled with sand, possibly a kind of substitute for food. The impression remains that the Omari people – like the people from Merimde – did not devote much effort to burying their dead, although there are some signs that the tombs were marked at the surface.[2]

From about 4000 BC a third culture developed in Lower Egypt, again so far identified at only a few sites. This is the Maadi or Maadi-Buto culture. Like Omari, it is a farming society, but with the sporadic use of copper (Chalcolithic, or copper stone age) and strong connections to Palestine. At Maadi, where the culture was first discovered, and at Wadi Digla, not far away (today both places are suburbs of Cairo), two cemeteries with a total of more than a hundred tombs have been excavated.

The burials are very simple. The dead are normally buried in shallow pits in a contracted position, laid on the right side with the head to the south. However, this is not a strict rule: many bodies are orientated to the north. There are never many, if any, grave goods. A single pottery vessel is most common; more than one is quite exceptional. Even by far the richest tomb has only eight vessels. Other grave goods are few. Sometimes flint tools are found, sometimes shells used to contain cosmetic powder. Copper objects, jewellery and stone vessels are rare.[3] Comparison with the excavated settlement sites, where many fragments of stone vessels were found, demonstrates that the simplicity of these tombs indicates not poverty, but

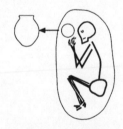

Fig. 4. Wadi Digla tomb 417: a typical burial of the Maadi-Buto culture. The body (sex unknown) is in a contracted position. The only grave good is one vessel (marked as a circle on the plan).

a specific cultic habit.[4] Grave goods are again not very important for the people of the Maadi-Buto culture. However, the vessels – most likely used as food containers – found in the tombs of the Omari and Maadi-Buto tombs show that these people did have some expectations of their afterlife.

Badari

In Upper Egypt the picture is rather different, as can be seen from the key site of Badari. Here the British archaeologists Guy Brunton and Gertrude Caton-Thompson excavated a series of cemeteries along the desert edge from 1922 to 1925. Their discoveries span all periods of Egyptian history, including settlements and tombs of the earliest farming culture of Upper Egypt, now named Badarian after this site. Around 4000 BC the Badarian people lived in small villages and buried their people in shallow holes at the desert edge, separated from their settlements. The bodies were placed in a contracted position, often on a mat. The head was

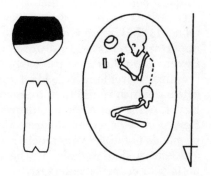

Fig. 5. Badari tomb 5710: burial of a child about ten years old. The body was wrapped in a reed mat. Next to it were a pot, a cosmetic palette and an ivory spoon (not pictured). Around the neck and wrist were strings of beads. The head was orientated to the south.

usually oriented to the south with the face looking east (towards the rising sun). Many tombs contained a few burial goods. Pottery is very common, one or sometimes two vessels being the rule. Other typical grave goods are cosmetic palettes of stone, used for preparing eye-paint. A pebble is generally placed alongside for grinding the pigment, together with lumps of green copper ore to be ground. The Badarian farmers were often adorned with beads made of a variety of stones and other materials.

The tombs do not vary much in size, suggesting that there are no major differences in wealth or rank between the people. However, some tombs contain special objects that might be interpreted as status symbols. In two instances a man was found with a belt of glazed beads. These are the oldest examples of glazing known from Egypt. Were these two men perhaps leaders of a village, or healers, or priests?[5] In contrast to Omari and Maadi, these cemeteries give the impression that burials were quite important to the Badarian people. The tomb pits are cut deeper into the ground and there is a greater variety of objects placed in them.

Naqada

Remains of the Naqada culture were first excavated by the British archaeologist William Matthew Flinders Petrie at the place of that name, where he found some two thousand tombs as well as a large contemporary settlement. Initially Petrie did not realise the true significance of his finds, thinking that he had found the traces of foreigners settling in Egypt during the period between the Old and Middle Kingdoms, around 2000 BC. However, shortly after Petrie's discovery the French Egyptologist Jacques de Morgan published a study in which he demonstrated that the finds from Naqada belong to a prehistoric culture.[6] From more recent research and excavations, we can today separate the Naqada culture into three phases (Naqada I-III), and date these to around 4000-3000 BC. This most important prehistoric culture is in many ways the foundation of ancient Egypt. The relation of the early Naqada culture to the Badarian culture remains a problem. Naqada I may be contemporary with the Badarian culture, which would then represent just a local variant in northern Upper Egypt, while the Naqada culture was developing in other parts of Upper Egypt. It is no great surprise that the burial customs of the Naqada I people do not differ very much from those of the Badarian people. The dead are laid in shallow holes in the ground with a few grave goods, such as pottery or cosmetic palettes.

The breakthrough in development comes with Naqada II, when the culture achieved major technical advances in arts and crafts, with evidence of growth of urban centres. Social differences become clearly visible. There are now tombs which might belong to a ruling elite, while others are relatively poor and clearly belong to the lower end of society. People of the Naqada culture still buried their dead in round or oval holes, but over time the tendency grew to cut rectangular holes and finally, at the end of the Naqada period, there are many rectangular burial chambers, deeply cut into the ground. This parallels the development from round huts to rectangular houses in the settlement sites. A few tombs were mud-plastered or brick-lined. At important centres of the Naqada culture, such as Naqada itself, Hierakonpolis and Abydos, many of these better built tombs (Fig. 6) were found at special cemeteries removed from the main burial places and clearly reserved for the elite of the regional centres. Some

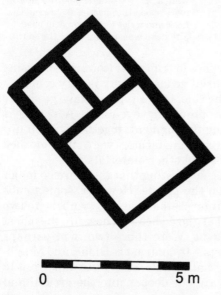

0   5 m

Fig. 6. Tomb U-C at Abydos. The tomb is built of mud-bricks. It was looted when found, but still contained a few objects (ivory fragments, amethyst and lapis lazuli beads) revealing the high status of its owner, who may have been an early king or at least a very important person of the day.

4

single graves have quite exceptional features, which makes it highly likely that they belonged to local leaders, the first 'kings' of these areas. One tomb at Hierakonpolis was decorated with paintings depicting human figures, animals and ships. At Abydos some huge tombs with several rooms have recently been excavated. The grave goods in one of these included large quantities of imported Palestinian pottery and the earliest examples of writing yet found in Egypt.[7]

In general, Naqada-period burial goods are similar to those of the Badarian culture, though with a pronounced trend towards placing more objects in the tomb than before. In the richest tombs at Abydos and Hierakonpolis more than a hundred pottery vessels were found. In this context, just one or two vessels must be a clear sign of a person of rather poor status. Richer graves also contain finely produced stone vessels, a highlight of contemporary craftsmanship. After the vessels, beads are the most usual finds, often worn as necklaces and bracelets. Cosmetic palettes with pebbles remain common, especially in burials of women. Flint tools and weapons are more typical in burials of men, though inadequate recording of the human remains in many cemeteries often makes it hard to determine the sex of a tomb owner. Particularly rich tombs contain a far greater number and variety of grave goods. Various amulets (clay and ivory figurines; small bull heads made in different materials) may have functioned as status symbols as much as for the protection of the dead. From the limited surviving evidence it seems that the deceased was buried in ordinary dress, although there are some indications that as early as the

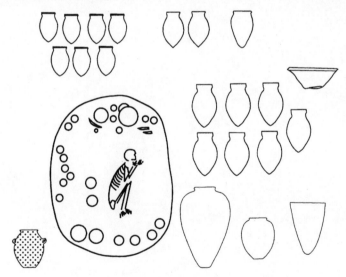

Fig. 7. Tomb 401 from the Naqada culture cemetery at Harageh containing the body of a man. The burial contains a set of pottery vessels, one calcite vessel (dotted) and three flint knives (not shown). The head is orientated to the south.

Naqada period the body was treated, the first step towards the future art of mummification.[8] Some bodies were placed on a bed, while other tombs yielded remains of coffins. In general one has the impression – especially for the bigger tombs – that many everyday objects were placed in these burials. Few settlement sites of the Naqada culture have been excavated, and it is therefore difficult to compare objects used in daily life with objects placed in tombs: vessels, such as painted jars, might have been produced specially for burial. However, a poor person would have been forced by lack of resources to place only essentials in a grave, such as some pottery jars for food to guarantee nourishment for eternity. In a rich tomb the same was done but on a bigger scale: the large numbers of pottery vessels found in some burials may indicate a wish to secure this eternal food supply. Everything important on earth was still needed for the next life and therefore placed in the tomb. Gender-specific objects such as weapons for men and cosmetic objects for women recreate the social identity of the dead person for the afterlife. Status symbols are important in identifying a person's place in the social hierarchy, and so must have been considered important for the afterlife too.

2. Early Dynastic Egypt: The Tomb as a House for the Afterlife

By around 3000 BC Egypt had become a unified kingdom, and had developed the features today considered typical of an early civilisation. Writing was introduced, enabling us to know the names of the first Egyptian kings and their officials. In all probability these kings came from the Upper Egyptian town of Abydos, where they were buried. About thirty kilometres to the south of modern Cairo they founded the city of Memphis, on the border between Middle and Lower Egypt. At this perfect strategic position the palaces of the elite and the temples of principal deities must have risen. Directly beside the city, on a desert plateau, the tombs of the ruling class of the new state were built. This desert cemetery zone is called Saqqara, after a modern village.

The burial customs of the First Dynasty are in general not very different from those already known from the Naqada period. The change lies in the richness of the tombs. At the end of the Naqada period, burial goods and tomb sizes became more starkly polarised. On the one hand there were now exceedingly rich tombs, with many burial goods and a complex funerary architecture, while on the other there were graves of very poor people with almost no burial goods. Egyptian society had become a class society, and this is clearly visible in its burial customs.[1]

The typical burial place of a high elite official at this time is the palace façade tomb (Fig. 8), a funerary complex consisting of two parts. First, the

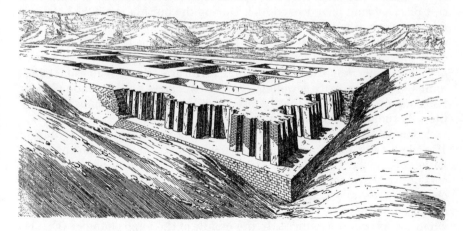

Fig. 8. Palace façade tomb at Naqada, early First Dynasty.

Fig. 9. Chamber filled with storage jars in the palace façade tomb at Naqada, as it was when found.

underground chambers reserved for the dead. These started out as simply a deeper shaft, a large hole in the rock. Later, in early Dynastic times, there might be an underground chamber reached by a staircase. Secondly, there is the superstructure built above the ground, over the shaft and the burial chamber. This consisted of a rectangular mud-brick block, with many rooms often containing storage jars (Fig. 9). The outside of this building was decorated with a niche pattern, also found on a palace or temple wall in the city site at Hierakonpolis, and in the design for the rectangle enclosing the name of the king as Horus. It is therefore generally assumed that the royal palace was the prototype for the motif, and the term 'palace façade' reflects this assumption. Such niche brick architecture is also found in Mesopotamia, and it is thought that the motif was imported from there. The overground part of these tombs included a space for the cult of the dead, though there are only a few examples of what such cult places would have looked like. During the burial (or maybe before it) the tomb was filled with many goods important for survival in the next world. Significantly, most of these objects seem to be taken directly from daily life, with only the coffin being specially made for the tomb. It is thus not surprising that excavators found furniture (Fig. 10) in the richest tombs, and many with jewellery, games, weapons and cosmetic objects. Food supply was the dominant concern, and in the biggest tombs there are literally thousands of jars containing food.

Tomb no. 3503 at Saqqara dates to the first part of the First Dynasty.[2] The identity of its owner is not certain, though the name Merneit was found written on two vessels. This tomb was plundered, but the looting was not very systematic and it seems likely that only jewellery and metal objects were stolen. After the robbers left the tomb, it burned and collapsed, so that everything under the fallen roof was quite well preserved when the excavators found it. In the middle of the tomb chamber (Fig. 11) was a massive (2.7 x 1.8 m) wooden coffin. To the left of it – its east side –

8

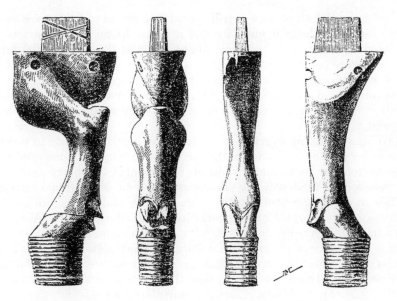

Fig. 10. Furniture legs found in the palace façade tomb at Naqada.

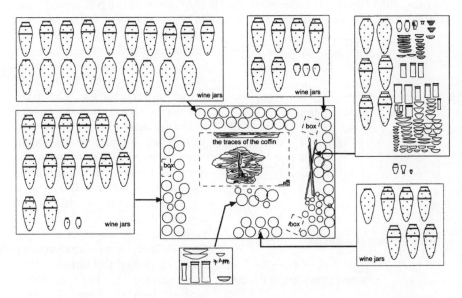

Fig. 11. Saqqara tomb 3503: the burial chamber. Next to the coffin was a set of calcite vessels (*below, centre*), one inscribed with the name Merneit, which contained the funeral meal. Emery identified Merneit with a ruling queen of the First Dynasty and thought this was her tomb, but most scholars now believe the queen was buried at Abydos. This tomb may belong to a wealthy person with the same name. North of the coffin (*right*) was a massive stock of pottery and alabaster vessels. Their shapes show that they may have been used as tableware. The small precious stone vessels (*centre right*) were the most valuable in the set.

several beautiful stone vases, still containing traces of food, were found. This must have been a meal for the dead as found to the east of the deceased in many early Dynastic tombs. Around the walls of the burial chamber were pottery and stone jars, and between them traces of wooden boxes were found. The contents of the boxes are not known, but the excavators found one ivory bracelet there, so they may well have contained jewellery. North of the coffin were three wooden poles, perhaps from a screen.

The idea of taking everything from life on earth on to life in eternity went so far that next to some of the big tombs at Saqqara huge mud-brick constructions for boats[3] and the burials of servants (subsidiary tombs: Fig. 12) were found. Evidently the people who served a high official during in his life on earth had also to follow him into his afterlife. There are long discussions in Egyptological literature about these tombs. Were the servants killed in order to be placed next to their masters, or did these burials take place after they died naturally? The question remains open.[4] Tombs of subordinates next to the tomb of their master are also found in later times, but there is no doubt that these later servants died 'natural' deaths. The First Dynasty servant burials stand out for their large numbers (up to three hundred next to the resting-place of king Djer at Abydos) and the great care with which they were arranged around the central tomb. In general the burial goods seem not very different from those in tombs of other people of the same social status. However, there are two observations to be made on the specific function of these subordinates. The first concerns the type of objects found in their tombs. In several subsidiary burials at Saqqara, objects in the tombs seem to point to a specific occupation for the deceased. In one there was a set of small vessels which once contained green, red, black and yellow paint.[5] This is an unusual find, which gives the strong impression that the burial is that of a painter. In another three model boats were found;[6] perhaps the tomb owner was a ship-builder or a ferryman. For others it is not so easy to see what profession they once had, as most flint or copper tools could have been used for various tasks.

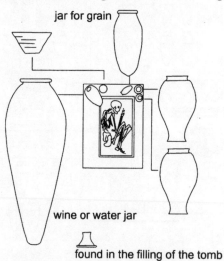

jar for grain

wine or water jar

found in the filling of the tomb

Fig. 12. A subsidiary ('servant') tomb at Saqqara. This undisturbed burial of an old man in a coffin contained several vessels. Typical of such tombs are the huge wine or water jar and the smaller jar for grain. Most of these vessels were found empty; the shape of a vessel announced its contents, and its symbolic presence was evidently sufficient.

A second observation about the servant tombs in Saqqara is the total lack of personal adornments such as beads or bracelets. There are mainly men buried in these tombs, and it is true that jewellery in general is not so commonly found in male burials. Nevertheless, personal adornments are attested for men at this time, so their absence may have something to do with the status of the tomb owner: perhaps a servant buried with his master was not allowed wear jewellery in his tomb. This is only a guess. In contrast to Saqqara, the Abydos subsidiary tombs did contain some beads,[7] but this is not surprising: inscriptions on stelae found around the tombs of the kings at Abydos and belonging to 'subsidiary burials' show that queens were also buried here. Jewellery may have been appropriate to the social status of a queen but not to that of a servant.

In the Naqada period and the First Dynasty one can already identify a tendency to replace some of the most expensive or large-scale objects with cheaper, smaller models. Some of the biggest tombs had burials of full-scale ships next to them, but in other graves there were only models of ships. Granaries are most important for the food supply of the dead, indeed a life-size granary was found in one tomb.[8] However, this is an exception and many more burials contained models of granaries. In the beliefs of the Egyptians, a model must have had much the same function as the object itself.

The burials of poorer people offer a dramatic contrast to those of the rich. A cemetery of the late Naqada and early Dynastic period with about two thousand tombs was excavated at Tarkhan.[9] Many of them are quite modest in scale and indicate how ordinary people were buried. The less wealthy Egyptian at this time had to select the objects which would go into the tomb. The smaller tombs are especially valuable as they reveal what was seen as absolutely essential for burial. For the simpler graves, mostly shallow holes sunk into the surface, the typical goods are again pottery jars around the body. In front of the head of the deceased there was often tableware offering the eternal meal for the afterlife. Many of the women and some of the men wore jewellery. As in the Naqada period, cosmetic palettes are common (though they disappear from burials in the First Dynasty). Other finds are rare. In some male tombs tools and weapons were found. In only a few tombs were there other special objects. In one such example, a box was found containing another box in the shape of the hieroglyph *sa* (the sign of protection) with an inscribed comb in it. Coffins are not very common in these tombs, but do sometimes appear.

During the First Dynasty the architecture of the tombs underwent rapid development.[10] At the beginning of the dynasty some of the bigger tombs had substantial chambers at ground level with a massive brick funerary palace, or *mastaba*, on top. All this must have been built after the death of the person. With a smaller-scale building this would have been no problem; but it is not possible to erect a huge funerary palace within a few days or weeks, the maximum time that could reasonably elapse between death and burial. In the middle of the dynasty a staircase was therefore introduced to give access to the underground parts of the mastaba. This produced the advantage that the whole funerary complex could be built while the tomb owner was still alive. Goods and the dead body itself could be brought into the tomb via the staircase after death. A staircase gave easier access to robbers too, so it is not surprising that many of them are blocked with heavy stones. Despite this, modern excavators have found that most of these tombs were plundered.

In the Second Dynasty the idea of the tomb as a house for the afterlife was perfected. While the underground parts of First Dynasty tombs consist mainly of one chamber, sometimes more, the number of chambers was now substantially increased. The underground parts of bigger tombs now look like exact copies of houses.[11] The burial chamber was the bedroom, and next to it was a dressing room, while in another room big water jars were found, which seem to indicate some kind of bathroom. Several such tombs have been found at Saqqara. In the Second Dynasty the overground structure of these large tombs became simpler. The mastaba was no longer occupied by many chambers, but became instead a solid mud-brick structure. The palace façade was used less and less by the end of the First Dynasty. Instead two small chapels where the cult of the dead could be performed are found at the eastern outer side of the façade.

The custom of setting up a stela at the mastaba is already evident in First Dynasty burials. To start with, their function seems to have been to announce the identity of the tomb owner, as they are inscribed with name and title. The most famous are the stelae of the kings found at Abydos, but there are also several hundred stelae there belonging to the courtiers of these kings (Fig. 13). In the Second Dynasty the function of the stela becomes more complex. Next to the name and title appears a list of offerings important for the afterlife. As noted above, by the First Dynasty and even earlier some objects in tombs had been replaced by models. The Second Dynasty went a step further, replacing the object by the written word. These stelae show the tomb owner sitting in front of an offering table

Fig. 13. Three stelae from Abydos giving title and name (*left to right*): (1) stela of the 'controller of the palace' Ip; (2) stela of the '(female) servant' Meres; (3) stela of the (dwarf) Nefer.

Fig. 14. Wooden panel from the mastaba of Hesyre, showing him sitting at an offering table. In front of him are offerings (wine, incense, meat) named in hieroglyphs. The hieroglyphs above give his titles and name.

with the offering list next to it. The words in the offering list are hard to decipher since at that time hieroglyphic writing was not yet fully developed. But comparison with later similar lists indicates that food, oils and linen are the objects mentioned. The appearance of food needs no further comment, while oil and linen are closely connected with mummification or related rituals.

The Old Kingdom starts with the Third Dynasty, which is in many ways a transitional phase: the goods placed in tombs are similar to those put into the burials of the Second Dynasty, while the tomb architecture, especially at the court cemeteries, is very similar to that of the Fourth Dynasty. King Djoser, the first ruler of the Third Dynasty, built the step pyramid at Saqqara – the first pyramid in Egypt. It was part of a vast funerary complex, with the focus on the overground parts of the tomb. Nevertheless, under and around the pyramid extensive galleries were found, filled with tens of thousands of stone vessels. Djoser's successors followed his example, but the size of the galleries was already reduced by the time of Khaba, who started to build a step pyramid at Zawyet el-Aryan. In the Fourth Dynasty there are no longer any supplementary storage galleries at all in the king's burial, clearly showing a reduction in burial goods.

Similar developments are visible in elite burials. While the number of underground chambers becomes smaller, the tomb stelae become more and more important. One notable tomb is that of Hesyre, who lived in the Third Dynasty under king Djoser. His tomb is a large mud-brick mastaba in Saqqara North.[12] The east side – the side oriented to the Nile – was adorned with a palace façade with niches containing beautifully carved wooden panels (Fig. 14) showing Hesyre in various garments and positions. In front of the palace façade was a long corridor decorated with paintings. These depict a series of items such as beds, boxes, chairs, games and other everyday objects. It thus seems that an important part of the tomb equipment was reinforced or entirely replaced by drawings of the same objects. The underground chambers in Hesyre's tomb are still quite big, and many fragments of furniture were found there. Apparently Hesyre had both an underground chamber filled with everyday objects and a mastaba above ground decorated with images of more or less the same objects. Unfortunately the burial chamber was looted, so we cannot really compare the list of items depicted with the tomb equipment. for. One powerful reason to replace real objects by depicting or mentioning them on stelae was perhaps precisely the looting of tombs, which must have been plundered from earliest times. People would have observed how insecure burials were, while objects named on a stela could not be stolen. Another reason may have been the observation that many tomb goods very soon decayed. Pictures and written words are thus in a real sense superior to the objects they describe.

From the Third Dynasty onwards, following the example of the king, the focus of development fell on the overground part of the mastaba, particularly its decoration. One important tomb which should be mentioned belongs to a certain Kha-baw-Sokar and his wife. This tomb has a small chapel entirely decorated with a picture of the Kha-baw-Sokar, naming him and giving his titles. Beside him on the walls of this chapel a long offering list is inscribed, mentioning all the commodities needed for 'life' in the underworld. Next to this chapel was another important innovation of the time, the *serdab* (an Arabic word originally meaning 'cellar'). The serdab is a small chamber in the mastaba housing statues of the tomb owner. This room was in most cases almost totally closed; there was only a small hole at a certain height in one wall to connect it with the tomb chapel. Through this hole it was possible for the statue of the tomb owner to observe what was going on in the chapel. The serdab is an important feature of many elite tombs of the Old Kingdom.

3. The Old Kingdom:
The Age of the Pyramids

Before we turn to particular tombs and the development of grave goods, several objects common in Old Kingdom burials need to be described. Coffins are typical of elite burials. They are sometimes made of stone and then more properly called sarcophagi, but more popular are wooden boxes. Although coffins become a more regular feature at this time, it must be remembered that most burials, particularly in the provinces and of less well-to-do people, do not contain one. Even in those that do, most are plain stone or wooden boxes. Inscriptions are not very common and record just the name and title of the coffin owner. The dead person was usually placed full length, lying on its left side with the head to the north. The contracted position was still very common, however, especially in the provinces and for people of lower status. Mummification was not yet fully developed; bodies were often simply wrapped in linen, though there is evidence of some special treatment in which the body was entirely and very carefully wrapped in linen, and the shape of the dead person, including limbs and head, was modelled. There are also examples in which the whole body was covered in plaster and remodelled in that material.[1] Canopic jars are closely connected with these first steps of mummification. For a proper mummification the entrails were removed, for as the softest part of the body they would decay most quickly. They were not discarded, but placed in special jars or in a box. These jars are known as canopic jars and the box as a canopic box. This custom seems to begin in the Fourth Dynasty. In the Old Kingdom both mummification and canopic jars are attested mainly for elite burials at the residence cemeteries.

Old Kingdom elite tombs consisted of several parts. There was the closed underground burial chamber, entered by a shaft or less often by a sloping passage. One burial for each shaft was the rule. There was an overground chapel, which the living could enter. The most common form such chapels took was a mastaba, a massive brick- or stone-built structure with one or more rooms for performing the cult of the dead. Some of these rooms, sometimes all of them, were decorated with pictures showing the dead person and scenes of daily life (see Fig. 16). These scenes often depict people preparing food and craftsmen at work. The most important feature is the false door, showing the tomb owner in front of an offering table which gives his titles and name. In many less exalted tombs the false door is the only decorated part. Another common type of elite burial has a chapel cut into the rock of a hill and sometimes (though not always) decorated. This type was popular in the provinces, although mastabas are also very common there. An important part of a mastaba was, finally, the serdab with one or several statues of the tomb owner and his family. These statues could stand in for the body of the dead person in the afterlife if that body was destroyed.

In the Old Kingdom, Fourth and Fifth Dynasty burial customs are very similar. With the Sixth Dynasty the world of the tomb changes, and that period will be covered in the next chapter. The Old Kingdom is the first classical period of Egyptian culture. In the Fourth Dynasty the great pyramids at Gizeh were built, the sole survivors of the Seven Wonders of the World. Sadly, all the largest pyramids were looted in remote antiquity and only a few remains of the contents have survived – enough, though, to show that the body of the dead king was placed in a hard stone

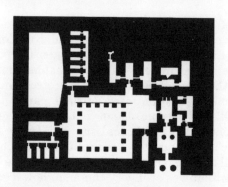

Fig. 15. Three mastabas of the Old Kingdom (not to the same scale). (1) Neferi at Gizeh (*left*). The mastaba forms one huge block with only small rooms in it, while the main areas for the mortuary cult are placed in front. (2) Userkaf-ankh (*right*). The mastaba is still a huge block, although a bigger room for the mortuary cult is located inside this block. (3) Ptahshepses at Abusir (*below*). The mastaba is no longer a solid block but filled with various rooms and an open courtyard. In general the number of rooms increases over time, but the three mastabas here all date to the Fifth Dynasty.

sarcophagus. In the Fifth Dynasty the pyramids became smaller and less well built. Their burial chambers have also been very heavily looted, often leaving only fragments of sarcophagi and canopic boxes. The burials of the high officials of the Fourth and Fifth Dynasty have fared far better, with a considerable number of intact burials surviving. Burials of less important people have been found and excavated in all parts of the country. It is therefore possible to give quite a detailed picture of the burial customs of the Old Kingdom.

Major surviving tombs from the beginning of the Fourth Dynasty show that the development (reduction of burial goods, increase in decorating the chapel) which took place in the Third Dynasty continued. Meydum is the location of one of three great pyramids of king Snefru, first king of the Fourth Dynasty. Some huge mastabas of the highest members of the royal court were built around the pyramid of the king. The mastabas of two king's sons, Rahotep and Nefermaat,[2] are particularly notable and

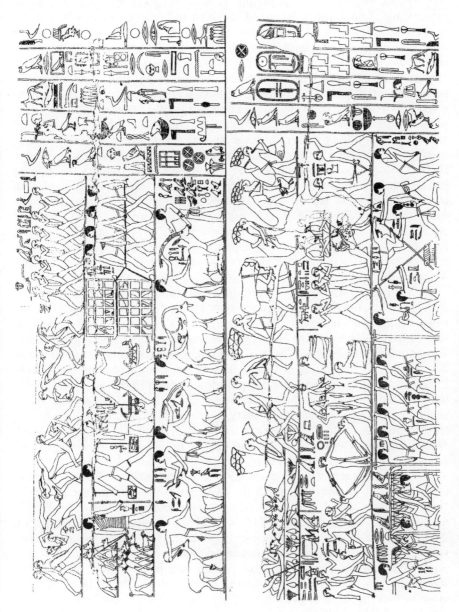

Fig. 16. Scenes in the Old Kingdom mastaba of Ptahhotep.

relatively well recorded. Simply by virtue of its size, the tomb of Nefermaat is one of the outstanding constructions of the entire Old Kingdom, if not the largest mastaba of the period. It is a massive mud-brick building measuring almost 120 x 68 m. At the east side are two chapels, one for Nefermaat himself and one for Atet, his wife. Both chapels are richly decorated in a special kind of relief, with silhouettes cut into the stone casing-blocks and then filled with coloured paste. The reliefs show a variety of people: working carpenters, farmers ploughing their lands and servants bringing food. It seems that these scenes show all the things that were important for the survival of the dead in the underworld. This may in part explain why the burial chambers of Nefermaat and Atet are quite small. Although they were plundered and we do not really know what they originally contained, it is obvious that there can only have been a very limited selection of objects. It was no longer necessary to place everything in the tomb chamber, because the chapel scenes show the production of food and objects which are thus secured for eternity. The naming of the most important things in the offering list had the same function: securing the supply of significant items for the afterlife. The tomb of the king's son Rahotep is no less impressive, with chapel decoration in raised relief. This tomb is especially famous for the statues of Rahotep and his wife Nofret, found in the serdab.

King Snefru built three pyramids in all, one in Meydum and two in Dahshur. At Dahshur many mastabas dating to the second part of his reign have been excavated. Their decoration is reduced by comparison to the slightly earlier ones at Meydum. There are no scenes of daily life, only servants bringing food for the dead person, who is still shown on the false door sitting at the offering table.[3] The underground chambers of these mastabas have been very heavily plundered, making it impossible to say whether there were also changes in burial equipment. However, the trend seems to be clear: the Third Dynasty saw a reduction in burial goods and their replacement by pictures and the written word. Under Snefru tomb decoration too was reduced: by the end of his reign there are no more scenes of farmers or craftsmen.

The development of tomb decoration after the reign of Snefru can best be followed at Gizeh, where Khufu (Kheops) built the largest pyramid. Next to this pyramid are the small pyramids and mastabas of his family and courtiers. The decoration of these tombs is even more reduced, with a single very fine stela in the offering chapel being the only decorated piece.[4] Only a few mastabas had more decorated elements, such as inscribed door jambs. The stelae depict the dead person and bear a short offering list mentioning only the most important commodities. There is no serdab. However, in the shaft of the tomb a single head, known as a 'reserve head', was placed (Fig. 17), always sculpted to a very high standard.[5] There is much speculation in Egyptological literature about the function of these heads. What seems clear is that under Khufu all aspects of tomb equipment were reduced to the absolute essentials. In the case of statues, this meant that they were reduced to the head, the essential part of the human body. This reduction in tomb decoration did not last very long, however; shortly after, or maybe even during Khufu's reign, mastabas were being richly decorated with reliefs – as in Meydum – and provided with full statues.

Fig. 17. Reserve head found at Gizeh, Fourth Dynasty.

All limestone-built mastabas around the pyramid contemporary with Khufu follow the same layout. They have no inner rooms, but there is a small brick chapel in front with the fine stela mentioned above. There is a shaft leading from the roof of the mastaba to the underground burial chamber, in most cases around 3.5 x 3.5 m in area and about 2.5 m high, the walls and floor covered with slabs of fine limestone. In the floor there is a rectangular hole, which may once have contained canopic jars, although this is not certain. In the burial chamber is a superbly cut limestone

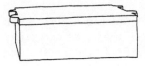

Fig. 18. Sarcophagus of a type known from Fourth Dynasty burials at Gizeh.

sarcophagus. All these tombs have been looted, and the few objects left can give only a vague idea of the original contents. The pottery is most important for revealing belief in the afterlife, with two main types: vessels of daily use and model vessels. Those of daily use can be further divided into two groups: Egyptian pottery and an amazingly high number of foreign imports, mostly from Palestine. These show the high status of the people buried here. Next to the pottery were found many stone vessels which can also be divided into those of daily use and model vessels.[6] The only other common finds in the tombs are flint and copper tools. The flint reminds us that in the Pyramid Age stone tools are still very common. The copper tools are often only models. From some slightly later undisturbed tombs, it will be shown that it is unlikely that these tombs contained many more objects.

The models of tools and vessels deserve further comment. It has already been seen that models appeared in tombs in early Dynastic times, when they often stood in for very large objects such as granaries or ships. In the Fourth Dynasty objects of modest size, such as pottery and calcite vessels as well as copper tools, were also replaced by smaller models. This kind of substitution may have several causes. A model is cheaper than an original object, although they mostly appear in tombs of those of very high status, who must have had access to many resources. Another practical reason, as we have seen, may be that a model was not very attractive to looters, though, again, even small quantities of copper had their value. This leaves possible religious reasons, but these are at present invisible in the absence of explanatory texts.

An important question about tombs of the Fourth Dynasty concerns canopic jars, which are closely connected to mummification. In Meydum several tombs were found with a hole in the ground that might have been used for depositing the entrails, though there is no real proof of this.[7] The same hole in the ground is found in the tomb chambers of elite burials around the Khufu pyramid. Here again, there is no direct evidence that these cavities were made for the entrails. In the tomb of queen Hetepheres (mother of Khufu) a calcite box was found still containing the entrails. This is the oldest known canopic box. For the rest of the Old Kingdom there is some evidence for canopic boxes in other royal tombs. They are in most cases sunk into the floor of the burial chamber next to the sarcophagus. In the pyramid of Pepy II the box still contained three broken calcite vases. In the Old Kingdom calcite or stone canopic boxes are not attested for private individuals, but there are some examples made of wood. It was more common to place just four pottery or calcite vases next to the coffin. These vases are of a simple shape, with flat rounded lids. Canopic jars of the vizier Kagemni, inscribed with his name and titles, date from the Sixth Dynasty. Canopic jars are attested for the Old Kingdom only at court cemeteries (Gizeh, Abusir, Saqqara).[8]

As stated above, almost all known elite tombs of the early Fourth Dynasty were found looted. However, there is one important exception. The burial chamber of Hetepheres, the possible wife of king Snefru and possible mother of king Khufu, was found almost intact. It was discovered at the bottom of a deep shaft near the pyramid of the king at Gizeh. The tomb contained objects of the types already discussed: everyday pottery, including some foreign types, model pottery, and model and full-size calcite vessels. There are also some golden vessels, jewellery and a head-rest. More unexpected is a set of gilt furniture – two armchairs, a carrying chair, a bed, a box and a canopy. Next to these objects was a calcite sarcophagus (which was empty) and a canopic box.[9] The items of furniture found in the tomb are not everyday objects, as one might expect, but seem instead to have a specific religious function. The canopy, bed and head-rest are objects often depicted in tombs of the Old Kingdom; they seem to have a strong connection with rebirth.[10] The two chairs and the carrying chair might have something to do with the status of Hetepheres as mother of the king, especially as they are covered with royal and religious symbols.

The serdab has already been mentioned: the chamber for statues of the tomb owner, his wife and his family. At the end of the Fourth Dynasty servant statues made in limestone were also placed in some tombs. The earliest examples are found in the tombs of queen Meresankh III and queen Khamerernebti; both date to the end of the Fourth Dynasty. They show servants concerned with food production: a kneeling woman milling is very commonly depicted.[11] The scenes on the walls of the chapel were evidently not considered sufficient, so statues showing the same subjects were placed in the tomb too. However, such statues do not appear very often in tombs of the Old Kingdom: not everybody followed this 'fashion'. Two or three servant statues are common in tombs which do contain such figures. The number of twenty-six in the mastaba of Nykaw-Inpu at Gizeh

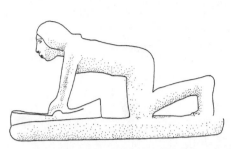 

Fig. 19. Statues of a miller (33 cm long, from Gizeh) and a potter (said to be from Gizeh).

is quite exceptional. In the Fifth Dynasty the repertoire of statues was enlarged. There are now not only servants involved in food production, but also porters, sandal-bearers,[12] a servant cleaning a beer jar[13] and one servant sitting next to a potter's wheel.[14] These servant figures normally show one person alone and are sometimes relatively high quality works of art.

An undisturbed tomb at Gizeh, dating from around the mid-Fourth Dynasty, may show a typical elite burial of a person belonging to the royal court, although this is not confirmed by written evidence. The burial was found in a chamber under a huge mastaba half carved into the rock and half constructed from large blocks of local limestone. The dead person was buried in a massive but rough-hewn limestone sarcophagus containing a wooden coffin. Next to it were some vessels and four canopic jars. On the west side of the sarcophagus were many small model copper tools, model copper vessels and a full-size washing dish set. There were also some cattle bones on the west side. Strangely the jewellery, in this case a broad collar, was found lying on the sarcophagus and not inside on the mummy. The tomb owner is not known. A statue found close to the tomb belongs to a prince called Babaf, but it is very likely this was brought here later. Sadly the skeleton of the dead person was never examined, so it is not known if the burial was of a man or a woman.[15] Taking into account the

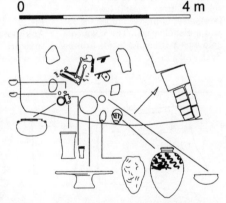

0   4 m

Fig. 20. The undisturbed burial chamber of an approximately forty-year-old man at el-Tarif, Thebes, Fourth Dynasty. The burial was found at the bottom of a shaft in a massive mastaba almost fifteen metres long. The tomb owner is therefore highly likely to have been a person of great local importance. His body was placed on its left side, head to the north. The burial goods include a decorated wine jar and some very finely made stone vessels (calcite, breccia, diorite). The skeleton was surrounded by chalk.

21

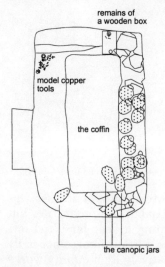

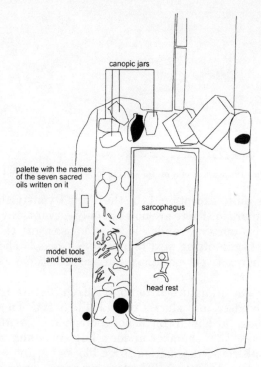

Fig. 21. The undisturbed burial chamber of Seshemu at Gizeh. Seshemu was an official of modest rank with the title 'overseer of the storerooms of the palace'. The burial chamber contained a wooden coffin, four canopic jars, several pottery vessels (twenty jars), a set of model copper tools and a model vessel. There was a gold wire with some beads around Seshemu's neck.

Fig. 22. The undisturbed burial chamber of Ankh-khaf at Gizeh. He was overseer of the 'double treasury' ('overseer of the two houses of silver') and thus belonged to the highest level of administration.

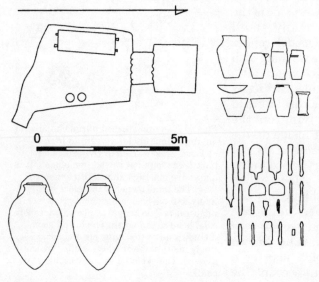

Fig. 23. Gizeh shaft tomb 316. This tomb, excavated in 1913, was found undisturbed. It had a medium-sized mastaba. The name of the person buried here is unknown. The burial chamber was at the bottom of a shaft seven metres deep. Next to the coffin several model copper tools and model calcite vessels were found (only the types found are depicted, not the total number of vessels). Two 40 cm high jars were leaning against the wall of the tomb chamber.

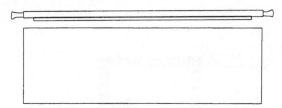

Fig. 24. Gizeh tomb 316: calcite table found on the east side of the coffin. On the table were pieces of bread and next to it were cuts of beef from cattle. These constituted the funeral meal.

Fig. 25. Gizeh tomb 316: the wooden coffin was undecorated and contained a second (inner) coffin. The inner coffin did not have its own cover or base. The skeleton was found lying on its left side, head to the north, looking to the east.

fact that the burial is the smaller one of two in the mastaba, it seems likely that the larger contained the tomb owner – a high official – and the smaller his wife.

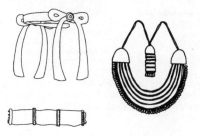

The developments described so far are typical of burials of the elite in residence cemeteries. Burials in the provinces, far away from the capital, are slightly different. A good example is the cemetery of Naga ed-Deir, which was excavated and well documented by George Reisner in the early twentieth century. Mastaba 561 was

Fig. 26. Gizeh tomb 316: the jewelley found on the mummy consisted of a gilded copper headdress; a partly gilded faience bead necklace and a faience bead bracelet.

found undisturbed. The brick-built structure on top of the burial chamber was about 10.6 x 5.9 m in area, making it one of the largest in the cemetery. The person buried here must have been a local leader. The underground part of his tomb could be entered by a staircase, on which two copper vessels where found: an ewer and a bowl, perhaps left there after some burial ritual took place.[16] The small burial chamber was blocked. Inside, the dead person was laid on the ground in a contracted position. On the east side were some stone vessels and a calcite table, the remains of the funerary meal. The whole burial makes a simple but not poor impression; the copper vessels and stone vases in particular must have been quite expensive.[17] The wife of the tomb owner was not buried in the same mastaba, but another contemporary mastaba was found alongside which may be her burial place.

Some intact tombs excavated at Gizeh confirm the impression that elite burials in the Old Kingdom were rather simple. In a shaft tomb about fourteen metres deep the burial of a young woman was found. Her only grave goods are necklaces, partly of gold. There were no other objects or pottery in her tomb.[18] Another tomb at Gizeh was richer. Beside eighty model calcite vessels, some pots of foreign origin, Egyptian pottery and the model of an offering table were found. The dead person – a woman – was

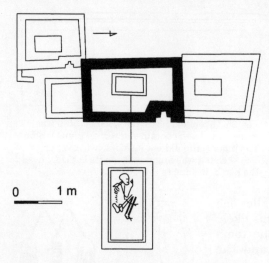

0   1 m

Fig. 27. Naga ed-Deir N 645: the mastaba (shown in black) is surrounded by others, which may belong to members of the family of the person buried in N 645.

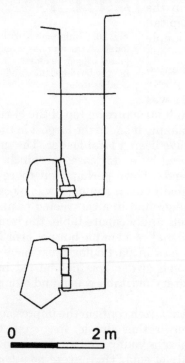

0   2 m

Fig. 28. Gizeh tomb 6041 F: the shaft contained the undisturbed burial of an adult man laid on his left side. The body had once been wrapped in linen; there are no other objects in the tomb.

laid in a huge limestone sarcopagus. Her body was adorned with jewellery, and special mention should be made of a gold crown and a bead net dress. A unique feature is a set of ten fingers made of clay, found with the mummy.[19] A boy about twelve years old was found in a wooden coffin. His head was adorned with a gold wire necklace and at his left hand were many model copper tools and weapons.[20]

Going down in social level, there are many tombs without any grave goods. Naga ed-Deir N 645 (Fig. 27) consists of a small mastaba (5.25 x 3.20 m) with outer walls built of brick and then filled with sand and stone. The small burial chamber (2.2 x 1.6 m) under the mastaba is built in mud-brick. Inside was a wooden coffin which filled the whole chamber. The body of the dead person – probably an adult man – was placed in a contracted position with the head to the south. The tomb was found intact, but there are no grave goods at all. Despite its modest size, the elaborate construction of the mastaba and the burial chamber shows that this man was not one of the poorest.[21]

A common funerary practice was the pot burial (Fig. 29), in which the body of the dead person was placed in a massive pottery vessel. In provincial cemeteries in particular, many people were laid to rest in huge vessels with lids. Since such vessels cannot have been very cheap, it can be assumed that those buried in them were not very poor. Generally only a few grave goods found with such burials, reflecting the general tendency of the time not to deposit many grave goods in a tomb.

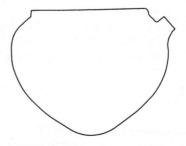

Fig. 29. This vessel was found on top of the burial of a one-year-old child at Gurob. The child was placed on a mat, with the vessel upside down over it. The vessel had been broken and repaired in ancient times.

Among the cemeteries at Gurob is one which was obviously used by a local farming village. 151 tombs are published from this cemetery, most dating to the Fifth Dynasty. The tombs consist in general of shallow holes in the earth. The bodies of the dead are principally buried in a contracted position, most often laid on the left side with the head to the north. There are many exceptions in which either the body was placed on the right side, or the head was oriented to the east. There are almost no coffins, but it was normal to wrap the bodies in a mat. Grave goods do not appear very often; one pot is exceptional. In some tombs beads were found, but some bodies had just one bead as the only grave good. Other finds are very rare. In one tomb a head-rest was found; in another a simple box.[22] Altogether, these tombs give an idea of the burial customs of a farming community. Bearing

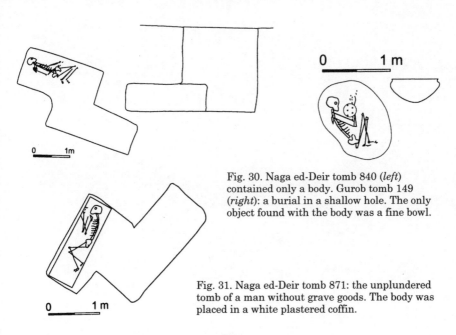

Fig. 30. Naga ed-Deir tomb 840 (*left*) contained only a body. Gurob tomb 149 (*right*): a burial in a shallow hole. The only object found with the body was a fine bowl.

Fig. 31. Naga ed-Deir tomb 871: the unplundered tomb of a man without grave goods. The body was placed in a white plastered coffin.

in mind that at this time grave goods are not very common, the people buried here may not have been the poorest, but simply following the standards of the time. Sadly, not many other cemeteries that might belong to farmers have been excavated, making it hard to compare the context and size of the tombs. However, contemporary tombs in the Qau-Mostagedda region reflect the same traditions.

4. The Late Old Kingdom to the Middle Kingdom: The Development of a Funerary Industry

The late Old Kingdom

New religious beliefs had emerged by the end of the Fifth Dynasty, with the appearance of the god Osiris as the key feature. In later times Osiris is the main god of the underworld. He is first mentioned in some offering formulae on false doors of the Fifth Dynasty, and by the Sixth Dynasty he seems to be fully established as one of the major gods of the afterlife. His rise coincides with the devotion of more attention to the underground parts of the tomb from the end of the Fifth Dynasty onwards. The first visible step is the decoration of the burial chambers of the pyramids. The walls within the pyramid of king Unas (the last king of the Fifth Dynasty) are covered with long religious inscriptions known as 'pyramid texts'. Prayers, liturgies and various kinds of spell combine to ensure the survival of the king in the afterlife. To start with, pyramid texts appear exclusively in the tombs of kings, but later (starting with the reign of Pepy I) queens too had such texts. The last pyramid with these texts belongs to king Ibi, who ruled in the Eighth Dynasty. In the First Intermediate Period private persons too used these or similar religious texts in their tombs, mostly in the decoration of their coffin interiors, but sometimes as part of the decoration of the tomb chamber.

There are numerous indications that new burial goods were introduced in the late Fifth Dynasty. Objects found in Fourth and Fifth Dynasty tombs at court cemeteries were very often specially produced for burial. However, these are most often models of everyday objects such as tools or vessels. In the late Old Kingdom tomb goods were still being produced specially for burial, but a high number of them were now not models of everyday objects, but items used in rituals or models of such items. Unfortunately there is no undisturbed tomb of a high official at the residence cemeteries to give us a full picture of such a burial.[1] Nevertheless, single objects survived in many tombs, offering a general idea. Some of the earliest burials with new objects come from Abusir, where most kings, members of the royal family and other high officials of the Fifth Dynasty built their pyramids and mastabas.[2]

In the remains of the badly destroyed mastaba of the king's son Nakht-ka-re, excavated at Abusir and probably dating to the Fifth Dynasty,[3] several calcite boxes in the shape of animals were discovered. In

Fig. 32. Calcite models of meat (*left & centre*) and of a bird prepared for cooking (*right*), found at Saqqara.

Gizeh tomb G 4733 E, a set of ninety-five small calcite models of food offerings was found, representing dressed birds, meat pieces, loaves and cakes.[4] In two burial chambers of the burial complex of the vizier Senedjem-ib similar calcite food models were found, but life-size and hollowed out, so they may once have contained the food they represent. Traces of linen show that these food offerings may have been wrapped.[5] Similar models were found in two tombs near the pyramid of Pepy II at Saqqara (Fig. 32)[6] and in a First Intermediate Period burial at Dara.[7] These tombs date to the very end of the Sixth Dynasty or even later.[8] Rather more common in the Old Kingdom are small stone model vessels. These are solid and usually appear in a set of several models together with the *pesesh-kef* instrument (Fig. 36), which was important for the 'opening of the mouth' ritual. They clearly have a ritual function in connection with mummification and related customs.[9]

Another important type of object which appears at the end of the Old Kingdom in several tombs is the model boat. Up to the Fifth Dynasty the custom was to bury one or more real boats next to the king's pyramid. In the mastaba of Ptahshepses, a son-in-law of king Niuserre, a huge open space was found, clearly reserved for a boat. Real boats then disappear from cemeteries, but in the Sixth Dynasty wooden models of boats start to appear in some tombs. These became very common in the First Intermediate Period, when they always have models of the crew on board, whereas the early models always lack a crew.[10]

Examples of late Old Kingdom tombs

The burial at Abusir of a certain 'sole friend' Kahotep, son of a Fifth Dynasty king's daughter[11] was not found intact, but still contained an amazing quantity of objects. The three hundred finds include numerous handles from various kinds of model tools (the metal parts of the tools were often stolen), a flint knife, two wooden tables, many fragmentary or complete calcite model vessels, a calcite palette with six holes, a similar palette with the names of the seven sacred oils,[12] four limestone canopic jars (at least one of the jars had not been totally hollowed out, indicating that it was never actually used), and fragments of boxes. The crucial evidence for dating the tomb comes from seal impressions, some giving the name of king Djedkare Isesi, penultimate ruler of the Fifth Dynasty. Two other finds in the tomb should be mentioned: a reserve head, which is quite remarkable since they are otherwise known only from the Fourth Dynasty, and great masses of mummy wrappings, showing that Kahotep was mummified in a special way. The body was first wrapped in linen and then covered in plaster, which made it possible to model the deceased like a sculpture.

Burials of the kind just described, including many models and objects used in ritual, seem to have been very common at the residential cemeteries (Gizeh, Abusir, Saqqara) whereas they are not often found in the provinces. Nevertheless there are examples of similar grave goods in tombs at important provincial centres. One such is a burial found in the Delta city of Bubastis, belonging to the 'leader of the palace' and 'sole friend' Mery-Merenra. This was found partly plundered, but still contained a set of twelve copper model tools,

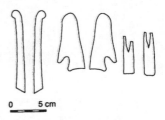

Fig. 33. Slate objects found in Bubastis tomb 161, probably late Old Kingdom. The function of these objects is unknown. They may have been amulets and perhaps reflect local burial customs.

some inscribed with the name of the owner. Other objects in the tomb were a copper mirror and some amulets. The body was laid in a wooden coffin. A pair of eyes might once have belonged to the coffin or to a mummy mask placed over the head of the dead person.[13] Mummy masks appear at the end of the Old Kingdom. They are most often modelled in linen and plaster (a material known as 'cartonnage') and present an idealised image of the dead person.

An fairly recent important discovery is the mastaba of Medunefer, governor of the oasis, at Balat (Dakhla oasis). Medunefer lived under Pepy II; several objects bearing the name of the king were found in his tomb. His huge mud-brick mastaba (18 x 25 m) was already heavily eroded when excavated, but the essential parts of the burial chambers were found undisturbed. Although its walls were much destroyed, enough traces were left to show that the rooms above ground inside the mastaba were once plastered and painted with the scenes of daily life known from so many other Old Kingdom tombs. The plan of the whole building, with an open

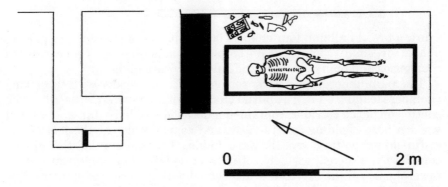

Fig. 34. Abydos tomb E21: section and plan. The deceased was buried in an uninscribed wooden coffin with the burial goods placed to the east. The tomb chamber was closed by a brick wall.

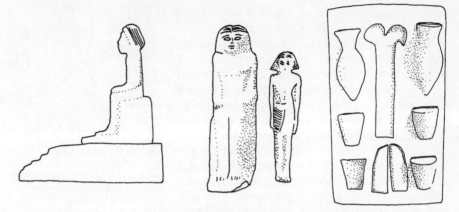

Fig. 35. Abydos tomb E21: three statuettes found lying next to the coffin.

Fig. 37. Abydos tomb E101: a burial in a chamber of a shaft tomb. The only grave goods are a copper mirror (found on the left arm), one pot and three stone vessels. The coffin was uninscribed.

Fig. 36. Abydos tomb E21: a model set showing the place for the pesesh-kef tool in the middle (missing in this tomb) and some small model vessels around it.

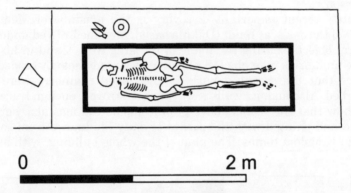

0   2 m

court, a broad hall and four chapels behind it, is reminiscent of a private chapel or small temple. (Contemporary mastabas at the residence cemeteries and many places in the Nile valley are different.)

The main underground parts consist of a long corridor with three long chambers leading off it. The burial chamber of Medunefer, situated on the south side of the corridor, contained a decayed wooden coffin and a set of wooden boxes holding calcite vases and copper tools. At the foot of the coffin many pottery vessels were found. The remains of the almost completely decayed wooden coffin revealed further important finds. Several parts of the skeleton were covered with a variety of amulets (Fig. 38), including a simple gold figure of a man and another figure of a man made of ivory. There was also a gold pendant in the shape of the 'million' sign (Fig. 38, bottom right), several wedjat-eyes in different materials, and

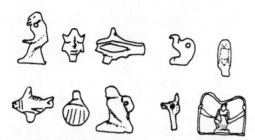

models of parts of the human body, such as head, hands and legs, often made from carnelian. Finally, there were many amulets in the form of animals, such as a dog, lions, a monkey and birds. The workmanship, even of the gold pieces, is mostly rather clumsy. However, this is one example of the growing importance of amulets in tombs. The precise meaning of most of them is still not known, though some, especially the animals, may be identified with gods.[14] In the Sixth Dynasty many amulets which will become very important in later burials appear for the first time. They are often made of metal (notably gold), faience or carnelian. They are first attested in the

Fig. 38. Examples of amulets in various materials found in the mastaba of Medunefer.

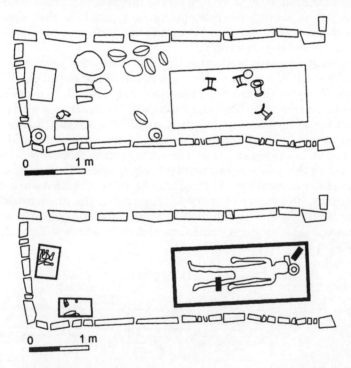

Fig. 39. (*Above*) The tomb chamber of Medunefer as it was found (north to the right). The coffin was already heavily decayed when the excavators found it, so the head-rests and calcite vessels found in it may originally have been placed on the lid. Next to the coffin were two wooden boxes and several pottery vessels. (*Below*) The tomb chamber of Medunefer, reconstruction showing the open coffin (with head-rest, vessel and two scribal palettes). One box contained several copper tools: the other, several calcite vessels. The original arrangement of the pottery is not known.

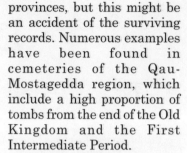

Fig. 40. Part of the mummy shroud found in Medunefer's coffin, showing the imprint of texts.

provinces, but this might be an accident of the surviving records. Numerous examples have been found in cemeteries of the Qau-Mostagedda region, which include a high proportion of tombs from the end of the Old Kingdom and the First Intermediate Period.

Another notable find in the remains of Medunefer's coffin were little pieces of mummy bandages bearing writing (Fig. 40). Funerary texts are only attested on mummy wrappings from the late Seventeenth Dynasty onwards – i.e. more than 600 years later. From close examination the excavator interpreted these inscriptions as the imprint on the mummy shroud of texts written on the inside of the coffin. Although it is not possible to identify the inscriptions from parallels, they are similar to pyramid and coffin texts, and they are the earliest evidence of longer religious texts written on a coffin.[15]

In the Sixth Dynasty it also became customary for private persons – maybe as a result of royal influence – to decorate the burial chamber, the underground part of the tomb.[16] There are two types of such decoration. In a few burial chambers at Gizeh the tomb owner is shown in a wall painting sitting in front of the offering table with an offering list next to him. These paintings are very similar to the decorative scheme found in the superstructure of the mastaba. In a few other tombs scenes from daily life are painted on the walls of the burial chamber, just like the scenes shown in the mastaba decoration. At Saqqara the tomb chambers are covered with long lists of objects necessary for survival in the underworld, along with representations of many food offerings (including granaries), and finally objects such as linen, sandals, head-rests and jewellery (Fig. 41).

Fig. 41. Wall from the decorated burial chamber of Idi, found next to the pyramid of Pepy II. Objects are depicted on several tables; a short inscription above gives the number of objects and sometimes also names them (in case their identity is not clear from the picture).

However, people never appear – the main difference from the underground decorations at Gizeh. While there are only a few tombs with this sort of decoration dating from the beginning of the Sixth Dynasty, many date to the end of the Sixth Dynasty and to the early First Intermediate Period.

Next to the pyramid of king Pepy II at Saqqara South a cemetery of middle- and high-ranking persons has been excavated. Several of the tomb chambers had this kind of decoration. At the moment it is not really possible to give a precise date for each of these tombs, but the cemetery seems to have started under Pepy II and to have been in use up to the beginning of the First Intermediate Period, maybe even later. One example is the tomb of 'the sole friend' and 'scribe in front of the king' Biu. His burial was found in a large mud-brick mastaba with several shafts placed next to one another; each led to a single burial chamber. On the west side of the building cult chambers were found, adorned with false doors with offering tables in front of them. One of the false doors belonged to Biu, another to a certain Pepy and a third to 'the sole friend' and 'estate manager' Henu; both these men also have their burial chambers in the mastaba. Evidently the building did not belong to one important person, but to several middle-ranking officials buried together. Most of the tombs in the mastaba are about the same size, though the burial of Biu seems a little larger and more elaborate than the others, in that his underground chamber was decorated: three sides bear pictures of various objects, while the fourth is occupied by the entrance. The south wall of Biu's chamber depicts a huge granary, clearly important for food supply in the afterlife. On the west the seven sacred oils, jewellery, a writing board, a head-rest, incense and several bags of linen are shown. On the east are the offering list and several food offerings. The whole decoration was cut into the stone and painted in bright colours. The sarcophagus was made from a single block of limestone placed under the floor of the tomb chamber, so that the floor of the chamber served as the cover of the sarcophagus (compare Fig. 42).[17]

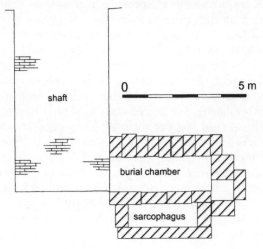

Fig. 42. The burial chamber of Wash-Ptah, excavated near the pyramid of Pepy II. The sarcophagus was placed under the burial chamber so that the floor of the chamber formed the sarcophagus cover. At the end of the chamber is a recess for the canopic jars.

shaft

0   5 m

burial chamber

sarcophagus

The mastabas at the Pepy II cemetery no longer include a serdab. The cult complex of these tombs consists only of the false door, sometimes with the addition of decorated slabs and an offering table placed in front of the false door. The statues, often made of wood and quite small in scale, were put into the burial chamber next to the coffin.

Other big mastabas at this cemetery are in general very similar, but sometimes have one important tomb shaft as the main burial. Nevertheless, while in the Old Kingdom each mastaba was normally built for one person and his wife, it becomes customary towards the end of the period to build huge structures with many burial chambers. The people buried here must have been in some way connected in life – for example a supervisor and his subordinates. This may reflect a change in the social structures of Egypt at the end of the Old Kingdom. The family was replaced, at least at high administrative levels, by other ties, for example colleagues at work, though it could just as easily indicate an expansion of the afterlife family from nuclear family to larger kinship units.

This focus on the underground parts of the tomb is evident at the end of the Old Kingdom in all parts of Egypt. An intact burial in Beni Hasan in Middle Egypt contained a coffin almost two metres long and next to it a finely carved wooden statue of the tomb owner. The only other finds are the pottery, placed at the southern end of the chamber. The wooden coffin itself was very simple, decorated with just a pair of eyes.[18] Statues in the Old Kingdom, as we have seen, were normally placed in the serdab of the superstructure, and this holds true for the provinces too. By contrast, in the Beni Hasan burial the statue stood in the underground part of the tomb. A similar observation can be made in the tomb of Meryre-ha-ishetef near Sedment (at the entrance to the Fayum), which contained an inscribed wooden coffin with a beautiful calcite head-rest in it. At the bottom of the tomb-shaft leading to the burial chamber a set of high-quality wooden statues was found including three images of Meryre-ha-ishetef showing him naked. There is also a statue of a naked woman and some wooden models showing servants producing food.[19] The chapel of the rock-cut tomb was undecorated, and there is no serdab. The whole emphasis was on the underground section. It is not possible to give an exact date for the burial, but it must belong to the end of the Sixth Dynasty. The nakedness of the statues requires further comment. From slightly later texts it is known that people envisaged a sexually active life after death. The naked statues clearly express a wish for resurrection with the sexual organs intact.[20] This view is supported by the statue of the naked woman found with the statues. She may have been intended to function as sexual partner in the afterlife, rather than being an image of a particular woman in the life of Meryre-ha-ishetef. However, the interpretation of these statues remains highly problematic.

The wooden models of servants in the tomb of Meryre-ha-ishetef are some of the earliest of their kind. Such objects became very popular in burials of the First Intermediate Period and the early Middle Kingdom,

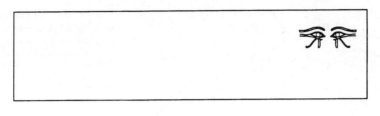

Fig. 43. Two typical coffins of the late Old Kingdom to First Intermediate Period (shown from the left = east outer side). (*Above*) The simplest coffin type was an undecorated wooden box. A common decoration on many coffins is a pair of wedjat-eyes. (*Below*) More elaborate coffins have one line of hieroglyphs with an offering formula on each side and on the cover. The eyes are always on the east outer side of the coffin. Hieroglyphs of dangerous animals are mutilated to make sure that they cannot harm the dead.

but it is hard to date their first appearance. The examples in the tomb of a certain Idu in Gizeh are perhaps the earliest in the residential cemeteries; several badly decayed models, including boats and workshop scenes, were discovered there.[21] The burial seems to date to the very end of the Old Kingdom.[22] A more precisely datable example is the tomb of Hepikem at Meir (Middle Egypt),[23] who lived under Pepy II. His models were placed in a small closed chamber, which also contained the statues of the tomb owner, and is therefore not unlike the earlier serdab. In most other tombs the wooden models were put beside and on top of the coffin.

In the Sixth Dynasty a new type of 'standard' coffin appeared.[24] Most coffins dating from before the Sixth Dynasty are not decorated at all. Even the highest officials are very often buried in simple stone boxes, in many cases neither inscribed nor even very well smoothed. During the Sixth Dynasty inscriptions, especially on wooden coffins, became common, and very soon a type developed which was used throughout the country. They bear one inscription on each side and one line of inscription on the lid. On the east side two wedjat-eyes are painted or carved into the wood. The body was laid in the coffin on its left side, head to the north and looking to the east as if to watch the sun rise (Fig. 43).

Moving down the social hierarchy, similar developments can be identified; more objects are found even in poor burials. Naga ed-Deir tomb 898 clearly belongs to quite a humble woman. Only a few grave goods (a mirror behind the head, calcite vessels and a seal) were placed next to her (Fig. 44). However, the seal and the copper mirror are objects not found in

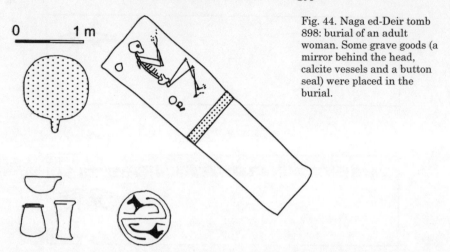

Fig. 44. Naga ed-Deir tomb 898: burial of an adult woman. Some grave goods (a mirror behind the head, calcite vessels and a button seal) were placed in the burial.

earlier burials. Badari 4903 belongs to another woman who lived in a small rural community in Upper Egypt. Her body was placed in a fairly shallow shaft tomb inside a wooden coffin, and may have been wrapped in linen (conditions for the preservation of such organic material are not very good at Badari). Next to her head was a mirror; there were some vessels around the coffin and at the foot of it stood a box containing some cosmetic articles. Some grave goods, such as the mirror and the cosmetic objects, clearly relate to the dead person as a woman. Of particular importance is a necklace with several amulets found on the skeleton. Some of them are gold and shaped like the hieroglyphic sign for 'million' (see Fig. 38, bottom right).

The First Intermediate Period

In the First Intermediate Period Egypt was divided into several political units. Local governors in several regions ruled like small kings, more or less independently of the central government at Memphis. This political fragmentation resulted in differences in the material culture which manifest themselves particularly in differing burial customs. Each region now had its own style in arts and crafts, as is evident from different regional forms of pottery. There are also regional variations in funerary culture, particularly clear in coffin production. Almost every cemetery with coffins is very easy to distinguish from other cemeteries by the coffin style. Examples from Akhmim (used from the end of the Sixth to the Twelfth Dynasty) most often have an offering list on the outside next to the wedjat-eyes. Those from Gebelein present unique forms of many hieroglyphs (Fig. 45). At Asyut, at the end of the First Intermediate Period, the text lines on the outside of the coffin start to be doubled, while at Saqqara the traditions of the Old Kingdom were still very strong in the

Fig. 45. Inscription on a coffin from Gebelein, First Intermediate Period. Gebelein is known for its many special hieroglyphs which have not been found elsewhere.

First Intermediate Period, so much so that it is often very hard to distinguish between late Old Kingdom and First Intermediate Period.

There are also regional differences in practice concerning the objects put in tombs. At Sedment it was common to place wooden models next to the body, even in not very rich tombs. The same custom is also found in the cemeteries at Qau-Mostagedda, but is not nearly so common. Similar variations occur even with the smallest objects. At the end of the Old Kingdom small round seals known as 'button seals' came into use, and are found in almost all the cemeteries of the period. In the Qau-Mostagedda region, however, they are particularly popular, so much so that some scholars believe they developed there. At Naga ed-Deir many tombs had a stela; similar stelae have not been found at Sedment or Qau-Mostagedda. One wonders if they have all been destroyed, or if the custom was not practised there at all. Similar stelae were found at Thebes and Gebelein, giving the impression that it was an Upper Egyptian tradition. At Denderah huge mastabas adorned with decorated stone slabs were excavated, revealing another local tradition. At Harageh two tomb chambers decorated like coffins were found. These chambers contained early versions of a coffin text spell. At the end of the First Intermediate Period weapons (commonly bows and arrows) appear at several places in tombs. Is this a reflection of the unstable political situation of the time?

Burials of the elite in the First Intermediate Period are very similar to those of the late Old Kingdom and early Middle Kingdom, and will not be described here. Burials of less well-to-do people in provincial cemeteries, however, do deserve attention. A good example of a place where a rather poor farming community buried their people is Gurob, already used above to illustrate Old Kingdom burial customs. In the First Intermediate Period the dead were mostly laid in shallow holes, head to the north. Many were

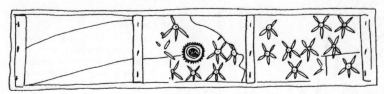

Fig. 46. Coffins were seen as a small version of the world. The lid represented the sky, the base the earth. This coffin lid underside from Naga ed-Deir shows the sky with several stars and a circle in the middle containing the hieroglyphic sign for town. This sign could also be read Nut, the name of the sky goddess.

Fig. 47. A copper dagger (there were still traces of leather on it when found) and copper adze from two tombs at Gurob, First Intermediate Period.

placed in simple wooden coffins lying on their left side. There are amazingly few grave goods. Many of the burials did not even have one pot; a single pot was the only grave good in other tombs. Graves with three vessels are exceptional, and other finds are rare. There are beads in several tombs; in a woman's grave a mirror was found; in a man's, a copper adze. Neither burial contained any vessels, showing that pottery is not always a marker of status – a copper adze must have been quite a valuable object. A third tomb, of a man, contained a partly plastered coffin, one vessel, a string of beads with a silver plate and a copper dagger (Fig. 47). The dagger must have been a status symbol – perhaps the leader of the village was buried here. Another exceptional find in another burial is a small silver pendant in the form of two lions face to face. The pendant is unusual in its design, and indicates the relative wealth of the woman buried in the tomb.[25] The First Intermediate Period tombs at Gurob contain only a few more objects than burials of Old Kingdom date, but the choice of objects is different. The dagger and adze are objects used in daily life; they were not produced specially for burial.

Tombs in the Qau-Mostagedda area of Middle Egypt are relatively rich and well recorded, but include the same range of objects. About 5,000 burials in this area dating from the late Old Kingdom, First Intermediate Period and earliest Middle Kingdom have been excavated and published. Many contained a high quantity of gold finds, showing the wealth of the region at the time. The richness of these burials has been much discussed, since it does not fit the conventional picture of the First Intermediate Period. The few surviving written records portray it as a period of political instability and social unrest.[26] Amulets such as small gold bird figures, carnelian legs and hands and button seals are typical finds. They were most often elements in larger items of jewellery such as necklaces and armlets (see Figs 48-49). The button seals metamorphosed into scarabs at

Fig. 48. Qau-Badari tomb 696, late Old Kingdom or beginning of the First Intermediate Period: burial of a woman in a simple shaft. Her grave goods include two pottery vessels and a set of amulets made of a variety of materials. The exact findspots of these objects around the body are not recorded.

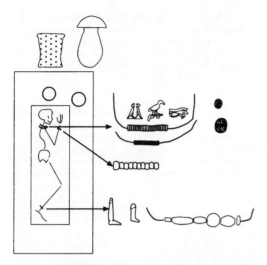

Fig. 49. Qau-Badari tomb 1735: burial of a woman found in a coffin with two pottery vessels (a bowl placed upside down on a jar) and a calcite jar at the head. She wore a necklace with several gold pendants (wedjat-eye, ibis, lotus) and scarabs (although the exact findspot of the latter is not recorded). At the ankles was a string of beads with carnelian pendants in the shape of legs.

the end of the period. At the beginning they are very often worn by women, while at the end of the period the scarabs are worn by men.[27] This suggests, but does not explain, a shift in function of these objects. Button seals were often used as jewellery, while scarabs are religious and status symbols that could be used in the administration of royal or private estates for sealing goods and letters. Men and women often have different objects placed in their tombs. The few tools and weapons are mainly found with men, while jewellery and cosmetic objects including mirrors, often placed in a box at the foot end of the coffin, are more typical of women. A high number of tombs contained coffins, but poor preservation mans that it is not possible to say whether they were decorated. Pottery and calcite vessels are common, as are grindstones. The latter are again usually found in tombs of women. It could be argued that grindstones have more to do with the status of a woman as a person responsible for preparing food in the home, rather than with the provision of food for the afterlife. Otherwise one would expect to find them in the tombs of both men and women. Few traces of food survive in the vessels or elsewhere. Most of the vessels were clearly functional containers for food, but the food itself was not put into the burial. A special vessel type, which implied its contents, was enough to secure a supply of food in the afterlife.

The Middle Kingdom

King Mentuhotep II, the first ruler of the Middle Kingdom, unified Egypt in around 2050 BC. Burial customs did not change much with unification; some of the poorer tombs described for the First Intermediate Period may in fact belong to the early Middle Kingdom. Typical elite tomb equipment was now a set of wooden models showing scenes of craftsmen and food production, a small wooden statue of the tomb owner, female

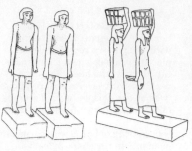

Fig. 50. Wooden models from the tomb of Gemniemhat in Saqqara (see also Figs 51-4), which was found intact and dates to the end of the First Intermediate Period or early Middle Kingdom. The body was placed in two wooden coffins, decorated on the inside with religious texts and friezes of objects. His head was covered with a mummy mask. Next to the coffin was a canopic box. On the coffin and the canopic box were several wooden models (others were placed on the floor of the burial chamber, but had been destroyed by the dampness in the tomb): statues of Gemniemhat himself and of two female servants.

Fig. 51. Models of a granary (*left*) and a workshop (*right*) including a smith, a potter with a potter's wheel, and a carpenter.

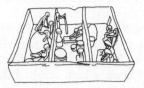

Fig. 52. Model of a building with people spinning and weaving; the arches indicate that the original building had a vaulted roof.

Fig. 53. Two models of buildings used for food production: (*left*) butchery, brewing and baking; (*right*) a brewery.

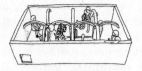

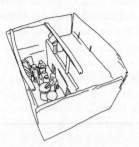

Fig. 54. Model of a rowing boat; the tomb once contained several boat models; others were placed on the floor of the burial chamber and have decayed.

offering-bearers and a set of model boats. However, there are also elite burials without these models. There are also wooden models of head-rests and sandals, most often placed on or in the coffin. Coffins are wooden boxes decorated both inside and outside. Other objects, such as canopic jars, staves, jewellery, weapons and cosmetic items appear sporadically.

Mentuhotep II built a huge temple tomb at Deir el-Bahari in Thebes, but few objects from his burial have survived; those that do include wooden models and parts of canopic jars. Around the tomb of the king many burials of his officials were found. In most cases these are rock-cut tombs decorated with reliefs, paintings or stelae. Sadly, the decorated blocks were mostly quarried away in the New Kingdom, but the few surviving fragments demonstrate their high quality. Some parts of these tombs clearly follow Old Kingdom traditions. The burial chamber of the 'overseer of the sealers' Meru was decorated with friezes depicting objects and religious texts. His sarcophagus was made of limestone slabs sunk into the floor with the inner faces also covered with friezes and religious texts.[28] This kind of burial chamber closely mirrors the examples found at Saqqara near the pyramid of Pepy II. In this period large fully decorated limestone sarcophagi become typical of the burials of the highest officials. Their decoration is almost identical to that of contemporary wooden coffins. Other sarcophagi are undecorated but may have once contained a decorated wooden coffin. Few burial goods survived the destruction of these tombs. One exception is a set of perfectly preserved and superbly executed wooden models found in the tomb of the 'treasurer' and 'high steward' Meketre. They were placed in a special chamber, a feature of some elite tombs of that time.

Wooden models (see Figs 50-4) showing manufacture and agriculture are a typical feature of many tombs of the First Intermediate Period and the early Middle Kingdom. They are still attested under Senusret II but seem to disappear shortly afterwards. The choice of scenes to be placed in a tomb must have varied over time and from place to place, but some kinds of models always appear. Other types are attested sporadically or even only once. The following list is a guide to the possibilities:[29]

boats
    rowing boat (Fig. 54)
    sailing boat
    (these are the most common models)
    boat containing the mummy of the dead person

food production
    man feeding an ox[30]
    man leading an ox[31]
    butchery (very common) (Fig. 53)
    man ploughing with a yoke of oxen[32]
    granary (very common) (Fig. 51)

bakery (very common)
fishing boat
brewery (very common)
woman carrying food offerings (a pair of these women is very common[33])
man carrying food offerings or household objects[34]
procession of offering-bearers[35]
man carrying a wine jar[36]

craftsmen and workshops
metal smith[37]
potter[38]
spinning and weaving[39]
carpentry[40]
brick-making[41]
shoe-making[42]
laundry[43]

others
soldiers[44]
scribe[45]
house models[46]
inspection of cattle[47]
men holding a sedan chair[48]

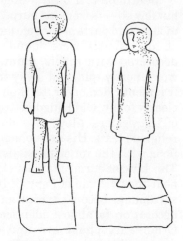

Fig. 55. Two statues found in a simple burial at Saqqara.

Wooden models were also found in relatively small tombs. A simple burial in Saqqara excavated next to the Teti pyramid held the skeleton of an adult placed in a reed mat. The only finds were two wooden statues of a man (Fig. 55).[49] Another burial in a shallow pit at Saqqara contained an undecorated wooden coffin. The grave goods were a pair of wooden sandals (only the bases survived) and a simple head-rest. On the eastern side of the pit was a niche carved into the soft rock and filled with a set of wooden models.[50] These examples indicate how common these wooden figures were, even in tombs of people of modest means. These burials also warn against making simplistic correlations between tomb size and social status of the tomb owner – a common practice in archaeology to determine the relative status of people buried in a cemetery. Without wooden material, which under different conditions would not have survived, both tombs would have been treated as belonging to the lowest social class, with neither pottery vessels nor jewellery. Although the people buried here clearly do not belong to the highest social levels, they could afford at least some funerary goods.

Examples of Middle Kingdom tombs

There are no undisturbed burials of court officials from the Eleventh or early Twelfth Dynasties. However, there are many tombs of middle-ranking officials which provide a picture of the burial customs of the elite. The tomb of the 'overseer of the storerooms' Wah was found next to that of Meketre, mentioned above. Wah was clearly an official or servant who worked for Meketre and was buried very close to his master. His burial was quite simple, with no wooden models, just twelve loaves of bread, a leg of beef and a beer jug placed next to the coffin. His coffin was inscribed on the outside, but not decorated on the inside. The mummy was carefully wrapped in numerous layers of linen, the head covered by a mummy mask. Next to the body lay Wah's jewellery: the outstanding piece is a silver scarab with his title and name as well as a title and the name of Meketre, maybe a gift from the latter. Under the head was a wooden head-rest and at the feet a small wooden statue of Wah and a pair of model wooden sandals. The quantity of linen placed on and inside the coffin is remarkable.[51]

A burial of roughly similar status and about the same date in the provinces, at Beni Hasan, is that of the 'sole friend' Antef. His tomb contained a simple wooden coffin decorated with inscribed bands on the outside. The body lay on its left side and was wrapped in linen, but there was no sign of mummification. Over the head was a mask; next to it were found both a wooden and a calcite head-rest. At the feet was a pair of wooden sandals, and on the lid of the coffin a similar pair was found. Both pairs of sandals are models which were never used in daily life, since they are made of wood, plastered and then painted. On and next to the coffin were several wooden models: a granary, two boats (a rowing boat and a sailing boat), a bakery, a brewery, a figure of a man leading a bull, and a girl carrying a basket.[52] Some pots were also found in the tomb. Only the head-rests and the pottery could have been used in daily life; all the other objects seem to have been produced specially for the burial. The tombs of Wah and Antef show the variety of possibilities within one period. Antef has a set of wooden models in his tomb, but no special jewellery, while Wah has a silver scarab and other expensive jewellery; the comparison reinforces the impression that at least the scarab must have been a gift from his master Meketre.

Twelfth Dynasty tomb equipment

At the beginning of the Twelfth Dynasty the court cemetery moved from Thebes to Lisht. With a different kind of ground, different local traditions and lack of adjacent cliffs, rock-cut tombs, common in the court cemeteries of the Eleventh Dynasty, were no longer used. In their place the mastaba once again became the main tomb type. The mastabas of the Old Kingdom and the rock-cut tombs of the New Kingdom are well-known sources for the court and provincial elite in each period. For the Middle Kingdom there are rock-cut tombs in Middle and Upper Egypt (Asyut, Beni Hasan, Deir el-Bersheh, Meir, Qau el-Qebir, Elephantine). These tombs are relatively well preserved, but they should not be taken as typical of the period. The normal burial for a court official was a mastaba at a residential cemetery

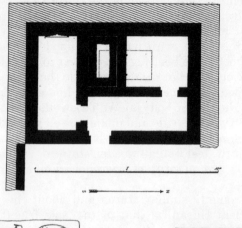

Fig. 56. The mastaba of the vizier Intefiqer at Lisht (plan: *top*). Little survived from the decoration of the Middle Kingdom mastabas. Here only the lower part of the false door (*right*), an offering scene (*left*) and some smaller fragments were found (not shown).

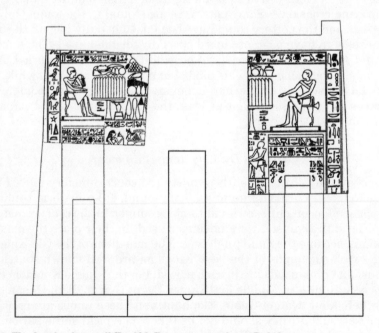

Fig. 57. The façade of a small Twelfth Dynasty mastaba at Dahshur.

44

(Lisht, Lahun, Hawara,[53] Dahshur). These residential tombs are today much destroyed and have never received the same attention as the mastabas of the Old Kingdom. One can therefore give only a rough outline of their development and appearance.

There are two main types of Middle Kingdom mastaba: those with inner rooms (Fig. 56)[54] and those without inner rooms[55] but decorated on the outside (Figs 57, 58). Examples with inner rooms were found at Lisht and Memphis. These buildings are often rather small, and decorated with a false door, similar to those of the Old Kingdom. Most of the walls seem to be have been decorated with reliefs. Since all these mastabas are very badly preserved it is hard to say if the decoration of these tombs was similar to the mastabas of the Old Kingdom and the rock-cut tombs in Middle Egypt or if there was a reduced decoration programme. These mastabas seem to be typical of the first half of the Twelfth Dynasty.

Mastabas without inner rooms have been found mainly at Lahun und Dahshur. They are often built of sun-dried mud-brick and covered with limestone slabs. The limestone façades are decorated with inscriptions and scenes showing the tomb owner with his family. There are no scenes of daily life. At least some of these mastabas were decorated with extensive autobiographical inscriptions. Some may have had a vaulted roof and two imitations of beams at each short end of the roof. They are quite similar to a contemporary coffin or sarcophagus. Some were decorated on the outside with a palace façade, imitating contemporary royal coffins or maybe even

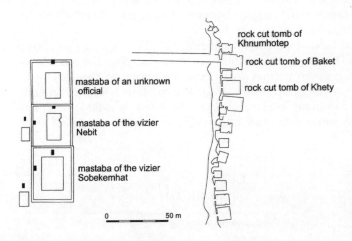

Fig. 58. Mud-brick mastabas excavated north of the pyramid of Senusret III, Dahshur (*left*) and rock-cut tombs at Beni Hasan, early Twelfth Dynasty (*right*). The mastabas are covered with relief decorated limestone slabs and surrounded by a wall. The black squares are the entrances to the burial shafts, which were placed outside the mastaba brick block. Some tombs in Beni Hasan are cut into the rock; the interiors are decorated with paintings. Shafts lead from these chapels to the burial chambers.

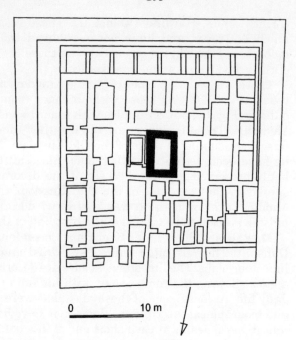

Fig. 59. Funerary complex excavated at Bubastis, Twelfth Dynasty. Each chamber was reserved for one burial; some contained the bodies of the 'mayors' of the town. The unusual architecture of the tomb indicates that there were certainly many local developments in burial customs in Egypt of which we have little knowledge. This burial-complex is just one example.

0   10 m

the Djoser complex at Saqqara (the prototype for the royal sarcophagi and for the king's mortuary complex in the late Twelfth Dynasty).[56]

The coffins of the early Middle Kingdom are quite similar to those of the First Intermediate Period. Decorated examples have a text line on each outer side. The inside is often covered with religious texts, friezes of objects, a false door and an offering list (Fig. 60). At the beginning of the Twelfth Dynasty vertical columns were added on the outside of the coffin, producing a coffin type with three columns on the long sides and one column on the short sides. A little later four columns on the long sides became common. In the middle of the dynasty a false door was added on the east outer side, and later coffins of the second half of the Twelfth

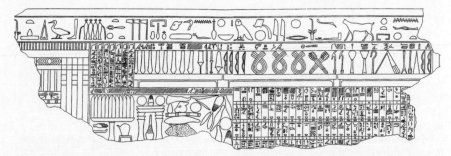

Fig. 60. The left interior side of the coffin of the 'chamberlain' Nakht, found at Lisht, decorated with a frieze of objects (bows and arrows, sceptre, etc.), an offering list (below, to the right), an offering table with food next to it and a painted false door on the left.

46

Dynasty were decorated all round with a palace façade. In the Twelfth Dynasty there are still many local differences in the layout of coffins. The examples found in Asyut and Rifeh always have double or even triple hieroglyphic inscriptions, while coffins found at Gebelein are often decorated with scenes of daily life on the outside, and similar decoration was found on a coffin from Edfu.[57]

Written texts have been always an important part of elite burials. In the First and Second Dynasties there are the texts on the stela placed at the mastaba. From the Third Dynasty onwards the mastaba was often decorated with several scenes combined with various texts. These are usually found only in the overground parts of the tomb. There are only a few examples where some kind of text is written in the underground part, the burial chamber. The only texts appearing there with any regularity are texts on coffins, and in most cases these are only titles and the name of the tomb owner. Offering formulae appear just a few times. At the end of the Fifth Dynasty the burial chambers of kings' pyramids are decorated with pyramid texts. The burial chambers of private tombs are sometimes, but not very often, decorated with friezes of objects. Religious texts, with the exception of offering formulae, do not appear in the underground parts of private tombs. They are also absent from the decoration of the mastaba. Certain religious texts seem therefore to have been particular to kings and queens. This changes at the very end of the Old Kingdom. At Balat, as we have seen, inscribed fragments of the mummy shroud were found in the burial of Medunefer. Few similar texts have survived from the First Intermediate Period, though there are many in the Middle Kingdom. These texts are known as 'coffin texts' and are often variants of the earlier body of 'pyramid texts', which also continue to appear.

Canopic jars underwent changes in form in the early Middle Kingdom. At the beginning of the period the first canopic jars with human heads appeared in the tomb of king Mentuhotep II.[58] The head-shaped lids are made of wood. There are also some lids in the form of contemporary mummy masks, which may show that the canopic jar could be seen as a sort of coffin, with the entrails inside equivalent to a mummy. These masks are always made in cartonnage – like the mummy masks – and always show a human face[59] which may represent the dead person. By this time, maybe even earlier, canopic jars were put under the protection of the four 'children of Horus': Qebehsenuef, Duamutef, Hapi and Amset. In the early Middle Kingdom Amset was a goddess, always shown with yellow skin and without a beard, while the others are often shown with a beard and red skin. Their names appear consistently from the late Eleventh Dynasty on canopic jars in connection with certain spells. Another type of canopic jar produced at this time is in the form of a vessel with feet and arms, or just arms, giving the whole jar a human appearance.[60] Canopic jars in the Middle Kingdom are often made of clay; high quality examples (mainly the jars found in the royal cemeteries) are limestone or calcite. A set of canopic jars is normal in elite burials in the royal necropolis, but not very common in tombs in the provinces. An astonishingly large proportion of the jars found at provincial cemeteries never contained organs.[61] For those who could afford it, it was evidently the custom to place a set of four canopic jars, including a canopic box, into the tomb without using them. These jars can therefore be termed 'models' or 'dummies'. Here a social class is copying a custom from a higher social level, without having the resources or even the knowledge to follow this custom through to its end (proper mummification). Mummification was not fully developed in the Middle Kingdom; the body was often simply wrapped in linen, though some special treatment is attested.

Single burials or burials of a man and a woman in one tomb are the rule in the early Middle Kingdom, but there are exceptions. In Thebes, the American excavator Herbert Winlock found three mass graves carved into the rock. One of these tombs still contained the burials of about sixty soldiers, who must have been killed in a war or campaign. Only two were placed in an undecorated wooden coffin. All the others were wrapped in linen, sometimes inscribed with the name of the soldier, and laid directly into the tomb. Since this mass grave was disturbed, it is not easy to say what kinds of burial goods were placed in it, but there are at least some weapons (bows and arrows). The tomb may date to the reign of Senusret I or slightly later. The find is highly exceptional, and must have something to do with special circumstances under which these soldiers died, perhaps in a Nubian campaign under Senusret I. Examination of their bodies has shown that all were killed or wounded in battle. This gives the impression that these are soldiers who fought for their king and were then given an honourable burial.[62]

Most elite burials of the early Twelfth Dynasty are very similar to those of the Eleventh and do not need further comment. However, certain finds suggest that at least some tombs contained personal items. Tomb 723 at Beni Hasan belonged to a man named Sobekhotep and is datable by the style of his coffin to the end of the Eleventh or early Twelfth Dynasty.[63] The burial contained an outer and inner box coffin, two model boats, a model granary, a model of a butchery scene, a standing female figure, a standing naked male figure and a pair of sandals. These are all typical burial goods of the time. Less common are a set of bronze tools and a bow with feathered and tipped arrows.[64] It is very tempting to assume that Sobekhotep's weapons have something to do with his having held some kind of military position. No title is recorded for him and no one buried at Beni Hasan with a military title had weapons in his tomb. The connection between the weapons and the military status of the tomb owner is therefore no more than a guess, but is supported by the mass burial of soldiers described above, who were buried with their weapons.

The grave of Mereri at Abusir contained a simple coffin with only one band of inscription on each outer side. The coffin yielded a head-rest, a staff and two wooden sandals. These objects are not exceptional. However, the whole coffin and the burial chamber were filled with emmer (a type of wheat). Another tomb at Abusir had undergone the same treatment, which must have something to do with regeneration and rebirth.[65] A similar idea may be expressed in some coffins in which the mummy was placed on a wooden frame filled with earth.[66] In the New Kingdom wooden frames in the shape of Osiris filled with earth and growing grain were placed in royal tombs.[67]

The main developments in the Middle Kingdom clearly mostly started in the residence cemetery at Lisht, to be adopted subsequently by the provincial courts. Two examples serve to demonstrate this. The 'treasurer' Mentuhotep, who served under Senusret I, was buried at Lisht in a sarcophagus decorated with a palace façade.[68] Coffins with such decoration are found in the provinces only in the later years of Amenemhat II.[69] This suggests that coffins with a palace façade were introduced at court under Senusret I and later copied in the provinces. The same development can also be seen with wooden models. Wooden models in the shape of the solar boat are first attested at Lisht under Amenemhat II.[70] Examples from provincial burials are dated slightly later. Nevertheless, such observations should be made with caution. The cemeteries at Lisht were heavily looted and are not yet fully published. It is therefore not really possible to give a full picture of this development.

The middle of the Twelfth Dynasty

In the middle of the Twelfth Dynasty certain new objects such as mummy-shaped figures, which will become very important later, appear for the first time in burials. Some tombs in the provincial cemetery of Deir el-Bersheh, datable to the reigns of Senusret II and III, are very important for these new developments, as they contain these objects and can be precisely dated. Although some of these tombs were found looted, there were still many objects in the burials – including a series of superb coffins – which reveal the burial customs at a rich provincial court. The tombs of interest belong to local courtiers and are all located in front of the rock-cut tomb of the mayor Djehutynakht, who governed the 15th Upper Egyptian nome for Senusret II and III. His courtiers are mentioned in the tomb of their master and may never have had their own cult chapels; maybe inclusion among the scenes in their lord's tomb was enough. Tomb E belongs to an 'overseer of troops' Sep and was found totally undisturbed. The burial lay in a chamber at the bottom of a shaft. Most of the chamber was occupied by the large, brightly painted rectangular coffin with inner anthropoid (human-shaped) coffin. In a side-niche stood the canopic chest. Next to the coffin were three jars. All other items in the burial were deposited on the coffin: two big clay plates, a brightly painted wooden table supporting three cartonnage vessels, a cartonnage offering table (Fig. 61) painted in bright colours, three model boats, and a model granary. The boats are of special interest as they are not the common sailing and rowing boats known from the early Middle Kingdom. Instead they clearly have

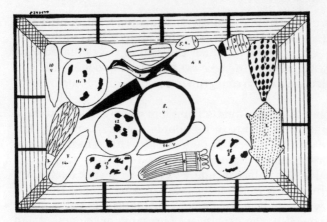

Fig. 61. Offering table
made in cartonnage,
with various offerings
painted in bright
colours.

some kind of direct religious meaning. One of the boats bears a figure of
the mummy of the dead person, another boat contains no people and
presumably represents the boat of a god, maybe even the sun god (Fig. 62).
The third boat contains a few figures of sailors and the dead person
kneeling under a canopy. The meaning is totally obscure.[71] A faience figure
depicts the dead as mummy and is very similar to later shabti figures (Fig.
63). John Garstang found an almost identical set of objects in the tomb of
the 'overseer of fields' Ma in Beni Hasan, precisely dated to the reign of
Senusret II. Next to the coffin were models of two boats, one of them
showing the mummy of the dead person while the other seems to hold the
canopic jar. The only other wooden model was of a granary. In this burial
the body was not placed in an anthropoid coffin, but had a mummy mask.[72]

In the Twelfth Dynasty the first anthropoid coffins appear. All examples
from this period are part of a coffin set, in which they are the innermost
coffin inside an outer box-shaped one. Most are made of very thin wood, so
not many examples have survived. Often only the metal parts have been
preserved. Two main types can be distinguished: (1) coffins showing the

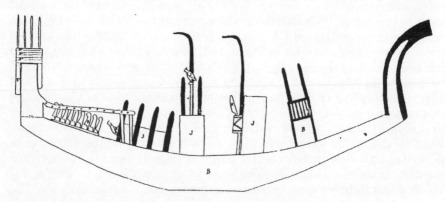

Fig. 62. One of the wooden boat models (90 cm long) found in the tomb of Sep at Deir
el-Bersheh. The boat may represent the ship of the sun god Re.

dead person with a wig, with the body coloured black or white[73] – this is the earliest type; (2) coffins showing the dead person wearing a royal headcloth (*nemes*) with the body decorated by an elaborate pattern – some such coffins are inscribed, giving us the name and title of the dead. A well preserved and documented burial with anthropoid coffins is the so-called 'tomb of the two brothers' at Rifeh. It contained two richly decorated box coffins, each holding an anthropoid one. Other finds in the tomb included one canopic box with a set of four jars and several wooden models. There are two boats, two female servant figures, wooden statues of the tomb owners and pottery.[74] The anthropoid coffins and the palace façade on the box coffins indicate that the tomb dates from about the middle of the Twelfth Dynasty. This date is confirmed by the wooden models. There are no carpenters' workshops, bakery or other models concerning food production. The tomb clearly belongs to a transitional phase when wooden models began to fall out of use.

Fig. 63. Deir el-Bersheh tomb D: a human figure in mummy form, made in faience. Similar figures become common at the end of the Middle Kingdom. Some are inscribed with the name and title of the owner or with short religious texts. The function of these figures is not always certain, but they clearly represent the dead.

Another tomb which may belong into such a transitional phase was found at Abusir. Four inscribed coffins were found in a small chamber. Two belonged to men ('lecture priest' Inimakhet, 'overseer of the priests at the temple called Mensutini' and 'overseer of the temple', Inihotep), and two to women ('lady of the house' Nekhet, and 'lady of the house' Satbastet). The bodies were carefully wrapped in linen with mummy masks placed over their heads. There are only a few grave goods. On the coffins were three wooden models of ships, and four pottery vessels were found next to them. Inside the coffin of Inimakhet there was a finely carved wooden statue, in the coffin of Satbastet a copper mirror, a bead and a scarab, while that of Inihotep contained two staves.[75] As in the 'tomb of the two brothers' at Rifeh, there are not many wooden models and no models of workshops. Another important point is the number of burials in one tomb. In the early Twelfth Dynasty the burial of one man and one woman (most likely his wife) together in one tomb is quite common, but more burials within a single tomb are rare.

Poorer burials

There is less evidence for burials of poorer classes in the Middle Kingdom than in other periods. Such tombs have not attracted much attention from excavators and have been inadequately published. The huge cemeteries at

Qau-Mostagedda mostly date from the First Intermediate Period, with remarkably few tombs datable to the Middle Kingdom. The burials of that period must have taken place somewhere else in the area, as Qau was still very important in the Twelfth Dynasty and it is highly unlikely that it was less well populated in the Middle Kingdom. The same holds true for Naga ed-Deir, where most of the excavated tombs belong to the Old Kingdom and First Intermediate Period.

The poor graves recorded are still quite similar to those of the First Intermediate Period (see Figs 64-65). The bodies were placed in shallow hollows or simple shafts. Burial goods normally comprise only a few vessels and some jewellery, including scarabs; women are sometimes buried with cosmetic objects. These are all objects taken from daily life, not specially produced for the tomb. The most notable difference from the preceding periods seems to be the spread of coffins, though these are in general plain wooden boxes. Riqqeh is one of few well excavated and recorded cemeteries with graves of lower-status people, with some richly equipped tombs as well. The dead were buried in shafts mostly with one or two chambers, sometimes with none. Each chamber was in general reserved for one burial, though there are exceptions in which up to four people were put together. A few individuals were just laid in simple holes in the ground. Burial goods comprise several types of pottery vessels and jewellery. One of the humbler tombs is Riqqeh no. 60, the grave of a woman in a simple shaft containing a mud-brick coffin and two vessels: a flat bowl, maybe for serving food, and a water jar. Tomb no. 63b was very similar but contained a drinking cup as well.[76]

The cemetery of Rifeh is known for its so-called 'soul houses'. These are models of offering tables and houses made of clay, found at the shafts of many tombs not only at Rifeh, but also at other places, mainly in Upper Egypt. It seems evident that these models marked tombs of people who could not afford a small mastaba,[77] although it is not really certain where

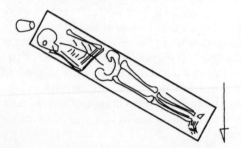

Fig. 64. El-Tarif, burial of the early Eleventh Dynasty. The buried person must have been of relatively low social status. The only grave good is a pot. The body was placed in a white/yellow washed coffin.

Fig. 65. Qau, tomb 409: burial of a woman in a wooden coffin, c. Twelfth Dynasty. Two necklaces were found around the neck. The contracted position of the body is exceptional for the Middle Kingdom.

they were placed – above ground, or in the shaft or chamber.[78] The soul houses can be divided into several types, but the main distinction seems to be that some are models of offering tables, whereas others are models of houses, sometimes two storeys high. However, they are clearly not copies of real houses, but rather show the most prominent element, such as a columned courtyard and the chair in the main hall of the house owner.

The burials of very young children and newborns still require much more research. From the experience of comparable modern and pre-modern societies, it is clear that there must have been a high rate of mortality for babies and young children, but they do not appear in graves in the cemeteries, even though older children do appear. The burials of newborn and small babies must have taken place elsewhere; cemeteries of infants were found at Gurob and Deir el-Medine. These missing graves are (at least sometimes) to be found in settlements. In one house at Elephantine the skeleton of a newborn child was found, placed in a vessel deposited in a room used for dumping rubbish. The body of the child was covered with ash, maybe to deter flies or other insects.[79] In another house at the same site a similar burial was found under the floor. The only burial good was a single bead.[80]

5. The Late Middle Kingdom to the Second Intermediate Period: New Magical Rites

The late Twelfth and early Thirteenth Dynasties

The reign of Senusret III brought change to all areas of life in Ancient Egypt. The king seems to have reorganised the whole country. These changes have long been recognised from the disappearance of the nomarchs and their magnificent tombs in Middle Egypt, but they must have gone much deeper. New titles appeared in the administration, some provincial cemeteries ceased to exist, and other cemeteries seem to continue only on a smaller scale. The body of the dead person was now no longer placed on its left side, but laid on its back, hands by its sides.[1] The disappearance of coffin texts and wooden models is noticeable. Evidently in the late Middle Kingdom there was no longer an industry producing burial goods on the same scale as before. Only a few objects were now specially produced for burial (e.g. the first heart scarabs, mummiform figures). In the late Twelfth Dynasty coffins became simpler. The outside was very often decorated with a palace façade, while there was no longer any decoration on the inside (Fig. 66). In the Thirteenth Dynasty the palace façade disappeared, and it seems that at this time developments in Upper and Lower Egypt went in different directions. In the residence region (Lisht, Dahshur) coffins are attested with four text columns on the long sides and religous texts in the space between. In Upper Egypt (Thebes and Abydos) the number of columns was increased. Some coffins have eight or nine columns on each long side.

However, there are some elite burials from this period that contain special objects. These tombs form a group, known as the 'court type',

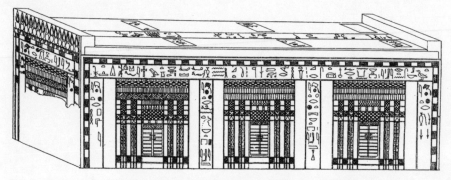

Fig. 66. Coffin of Ibi decorated with a palace façade, late Twelfth Dynasty.

54

showing that at least at the highest level similar rites and funerary goods were used. The type is mainly known from several undisturbed tombs of princesses and noblewomen, found next to the pyramids of the Twelfth Dynasty. There is enough evidence to show that burials of this kind were practised almost everywhere, but most often in the residential cemeteries.[2] A typical 'court type' burial can be described as follows: the body of the dead person was placed in an anthropoid coffin or adorned with a mummy mask, which was put in a second box-shaped coffin often covered with inscribed bands of gold leaf. Finally there was a third outer coffin made of wood or stone. Inside the coffins, right next to the body of the dead, were sceptres, weapons and other mainly royal insignia. Royal insignia were also found in other parts of the burial. The anthropoid coffin or mummy mask was decorated with the royal 'nemes' head-dress and sometimes even adorned with a uraeus (snake symbol), indicating that the body was identified with Osiris, ruler of the underworld, who also once ruled Egypt. Inside the coffin there were often superb works of jewellery specially made for the burial. Outside the coffin set stood a canopic box containing the four canopic jars. There was also a box with seven vessels for the seven sacred oils and a great quantity of pottery, consisting mostly of very small vessels and plates, more symbolic than practical. In the burial chamber was a second box containing royal insignia and weapons. As well as this typical equipment, each 'court type' tomb contained a selection of objects that distinguishes it from the rest. The burial of the 'king's daughter' Neferuptah included a set of three inscribed silver vessels. The tomb of the 'overseer of the storeroom' Iunefer at Hawara yielded mummiform figures (very similar to later shabtis), and the two coffins of the 'chief lector priest' Sesenebenef, excavated at Lisht, were covered with religious texts, a custom which was no longer current in the late Middle Kingdom. 'Court type' burials do not appear very often and are attested only for the highest elite. Almost all the objects found in these tombs were specially made for burial. The earliest examples belong to four princesses buried next to the pyramid of Amenemhat II, while the last known example of a 'court type' burial may be princess Nub-hetepti-khered, placed next to king Hor of the early Thirteenth Dynasty and doubtless dating to about the same time.

The tomb of king Awibre Hor is quite well preserved (Fig. 67). It is the earliest royal tomb to survive almost intact. The king was buried in a shaft next to the pyramid of king Amenemhat III in Dahshur. Since Awibre Hor reigned for less than a year he cannot have had much time to prepare for his burial as king. His tomb is therefore highly likely to be a re-used (or unused) shaft tomb cut next to the pyramid during the reign of king Amenemhat III. It consists of a small shaft leading to a corridor occupied by a huge wooden shrine that contains an almost life-size wooden statue of the king. This image represents his *ka*, since it has the ka-sign on its head, although the sign is not shown in the published plan of the tomb and has perhaps been put on the statue by Egyptologists for display in the

Fig. 67. Plan of the tomb of king Awibre Hor, Thirteenth Dynasty.

museum. Dieter Arnold has argued that this is a statue type normally installed in a special chamber, which in this case was put in a corridor because the king did not have time to build a full tomb.[3] The corridor with the shrine leads to the burial chamber, which was totally occupied by the sarcophagus containing a partly gilded wooden coffin, in which the mummy with a mask was placed. The mummy was adorned with several items of jewellery, and many wooden staves and sceptres were found next to it (Fig. 68). A long wooden box found beside the shrine contained a similar range of objects. In a niche at the foot end of the sarcophagus was a canopic box containing the four canopic jars. The burial of the king is in

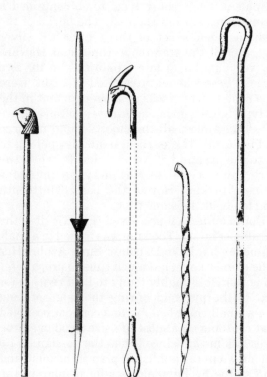

Fig. 68. A set of staves found in the tomb of king Awibre Hor. Similar staves are common in all 'court type' tombs.

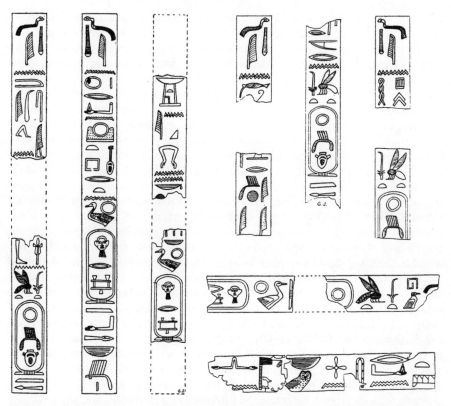

Fig. 69. Inscriptions in gold leaf on the coffin of king Awibre Hor. The hieroglyphs of animals and birds are mutilated, a practice common in burial contexts in the First Intermediate Period and again in the Late Middle Kingdom and Second Intermediate Period.

many respects similar to other 'court type' burials of the late Middle Kingdom, but there are some finds which are not found in tombs of private persons of the same period. There are two stelae inscribed with religious texts, unique among Middle Kingdom burials. The larger of the two bears parts of the so-called pyramid texts, while the smaller one has an offering formula on it. There is a set of wooden model vessels of a type not known from other private tombs, and a special vessel only known from royal tombs.[4]

Tombs not belonging to the 'court type' contained a different range of objects, quite often magical items. The combination of these objects varies from tomb to tomb, and it is hard to distinguish any rules. There are small statues of animals, most famously faience figures of hippopotami, but also in other materials and of other animals such as dogs, cats and apes.[5] Tombs often contained stylised figurines of naked women. Finally there are knife-shaped amulets of ivory, also called 'magical wands'. These new types of object appear only sporadically in tombs of the late Twelfth and Thirteenth Dynasties, and one gets the impression that not everyone followed the new customs. Closer investigation reveals that many of these objects are also well known from settlement sites; these are the magical objects used in daily life to protect against evil spirits.[6] Coffins are no longer inscribed to the same degree with religious texts, and instead some people put papyrus texts into their burials. These are not always religious:[7] many of the known literary compositions of the Middle Kingdom were preserved written on papyri found in burials. Another major change is that from single or double burials to multiple ones. Throughout Predynastic Egypt, the Old Kingdom and the early Middle Kingdom, one person per burial was the rule. There are already several exceptions from the Predynastic Period, First Intermediate Period and early Middle Kingdom, when it became common to place husband and wife in a single tomb. In the late Middle Kingdom many tombs were used for numerous burials. They must have been opened repeatedly to insert new coffins, mummies or just bodies. Objects associated with each burial became mixed with older items, and the archaeologist thus often finds it hard to tell which object belonged to which burial. The new custom was not followed by everyone; there are still many single burials at all social levels. However, even in the pyramid of Amenemhat III at Hawara his daughter was placed next to the king's sarcophagus. Princesses and queens of Senusret III were laid to rest together in a big gallery tomb alongside the king's pyramid at Dahshur. Only very poor people without the resources to dig a rock-cut burial chamber seem to have been buried regularly in single tombs. Finally, there might be local variants. While at some places, such as Harageh or Thebes, multiple burials are well attested, elsewhere, such as Qau in Upper Egypt, such burials are not very common.

The relatively well preserved burial of an official of the early Thirteenth Dynasty has been excavated at Thebes. The 'great one of the Tens of Upper Egypt' Renseneb was laid to rest in a shaft with two chambers containing at least five bodies. The objects found indicate the high status of these people. There was a finely crafted box with a depiction of the 'hall-keeper' Kemni offering in front of king Amenemhat IV, which may have been a present from the king to this official. It is not clear whether Kemni was also buried in this tomb or whether the box was a present from him to Renseneb or another person. The coffin of Renseneb himself was very much decayed. The remains showed that it was once painted with yellow mutilated hieroglyphs, a typical late Middle Kingdom treatment of hieroglyphic signs for animals and birds (compare Fig. 69). The custom of mutilating hieroglyphs started under Amenemhat III and is attested throughout the following period; it was intended to ensure that these animals could not harm the dead. Renseneb's mummy lay on its side and was much decayed. It had a cartonnage mask over the head and shoulders, with a gilt face. Inside the wrappings a blue faience hippopotamus was found, while around the neck there was a gold and obsidian necklace and an amulet in form of a shen-ring (a hieroglyphic sign for protection) (Fig.

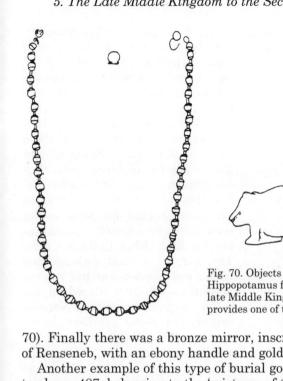

Fig. 70. Objects found in the coffin of Renseneb. Hippopotamus figures made in faience are a typical late Middle Kingdom funerary good. This tomb provides one of the few examples found in context.

70). Finally there was a bronze mirror, inscribed with the title and name of Renseneb, with an ebony handle and gold inlay.[8]

Another example of this type of burial goods was found in Beni Hasan tomb no. 487, belonging to the 'mistress of the house' Seneb, daughter of Iti. It is not clear from the excavation report whether the tomb was untouched or only partly looted, but there were certainly many objects left, which offer an impression of the original contents. As far as one can tell from the published records, the burial lay in a small chamber. The heavily decayed coffin was placed on one side of the chamber. Next to it were four big storage jars, of a shape typical of the late Twelfth Dynasty. At the wall opposite the coffin stood several boxes containing cosmetic items, as well as several stone vessels and two clay models of human figures.[9] On the mummy (which had a mummy mask) were several items of jewellery: two fish made of silver and electrum, a scarab, silver bracelets, lion-shaped silver pendants and several beads made of precious stones.[10] Seneb was obviously not a poor woman. The jewellery is of the highest quality. However, all objects found in her tomb seem to be objects from daily life, with nothing except the coffin and the mummy mask especially made for burial. The only other exception may be the two clay figures, but these are hardly comparable with the wooden models known from earlier Middle Kingdom burials. Similar figures, often in limestone, are found in other tombs of the late Middle Kingdom.

A well preserved multiple burial of some not very well-to-do people has been excavated at Thebes (Fig. 71). Five undecorated coffins were found in a small, fairly shallow shaft tomb. A sixth coffin, lying under the others, was destroyed, indicating that the first burial was quite old when the

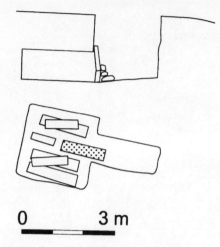

0   3 m

Fig. 71. Late Middle Kingdom multiple
burial in Thebes.

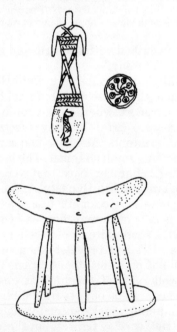

Fig. 72. Finds from one of the burials (the
coffin dotted in Fig. 71). The head-rest
(*below*) was found on the left side of the
head of the deceased, who was a tall person,
placed slightly contracted in the coffin. At
one finger was a ring decorated with the
pattern shown here (*above right*). Next to
his coffin and the other coffins were five flat
wooden dolls (one shown *above left*).

others were placed in the chamber.
Finally there was the burial of a
child without a coffin. Burial goods
were found everywhere; around the
coffins lay many pottery jars and
wooden female dolls with hair in the
form of strings of small mud pellets
(see Fig. 72). The function of these
'dolls' is very much disputed. Are
they dolls for children? Are they
concubines for men in the afterlife?
Are they for women, to guarantee
continued sexual function, or for
both sexes, as a general guarantee
of new life? Other finds are rare.
The body of a child was adorned
with many amulets and had a set of
miniature furniture placed on the
coffin. In two coffins a head-rest was
found. On some of them lay a
wooden staff, which may have been
a symbol of status. The bodies of the
dead were not mummified but
covered with sheets of linen.[11] It is
very hard to say to what social level
these people belonged. There are no
inscriptions which could give us a
title or any other clue. If they were
not part of the administrative elite,
they may have been a family of
craftsmen or farmers.

Few other lower-class tombs or
cemeteries of the late Middle
Kingdom have been excavated and
recorded. The archaeologist
Reginald Engelbach described such
tombs at Harageh but did not
publish them in detail: 'Wady I and
Wady II are two series of shallow
graves packed tightly into the soft
sand .... They appear to have been
the graves of the poorer classes from
the time of Senusret II down to the
end of the Hyksos period. They were
packed as closely as possible, and I
have had to omit showing many

60

groups of pottery and beads, as, in some cases, it was not possible to separate the burials.'[12]

Other cemeteries of to the late Middle Kingdom and Second Intermediate Period were excavated at Qau-Mostagedda, where most graves were reserved for just one person. The dead are most often placed on their left side with their head to the north in shafts on average only one metre deep. Burial goods are again few. There are glazed beads and shell rings and some pottery, although many burials did not contain any pots; other finds such as calcite or faience vessels are very rare. Coffins are not very common, but this may be the result of bad conditions for preservation: any coffin is likely to have disappeared without trace.[13]

The Second Intermediate Period

At some point in the Second Intermediate Period (late Thirteenth to Seventeenth Dynasty) the court moved south from the Memphis-Fayum area. The political history of the time is still very unclear. During the Second Intermediate Period many foreigners settled in Egypt – a Middle Bronze Age Palestinian people, known as the Hyksos in the north; Nubians in the south. Their burial customs are different from those of contemporary Egyptians. Tell el-Daba, ancient Avaris, was the capital of the Hyksos empire or kingdom. Many tombs have been excavated there, most of them belonging to Palestinian Bronze Age people, some to Egyptians or Palestinian people buried like Egyptians. One of the latter is of a young woman placed in a limestone sarcophagus. The only burial goods are a bead necklace and a calcite vessel placed near the head. Outside the sarcophagus was a further vessel which may also belong to the burial (Fig. 73). The sarcophagus indicates that the woman was relatively wealthy. In stark contrast to such a simple burial are the tombs of the Palestinian Bronze Age people. The dead are often placed in mud-brick built chambers. Coffins are not very common but do appear. The tombs are often richly equipped with burial goods, the most common of which are various kinds of pottery vessel. Animal bones in the tombs indicate that food was placed there. For women several kinds of jewellery is attested, especially scarabs, while men often have weapons and scarabs too. Burials of donkeys were found next to some rich tombs, near the entrance of the burial chamber. Altogether it might be said that food supply for the dead (vessels and animal bones) was the crucial feature. Other finds such as weapons and jewellery point to the status and function of the deceased in society. Weapons are not very common in contemporary Egyptian tombs.

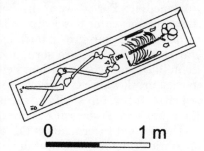

Fig. 73. Burial of a young woman at Tell el-Daba.

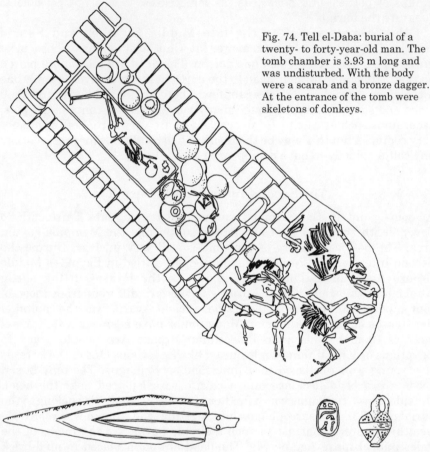

Fig. 74. Tell el-Daba: burial of a twenty- to forty-year-old man. The tomb chamber is 3.93 m long and was undisturbed. With the body were a scarab and a bronze dagger. At the entrance of the tomb were skeletons of donkeys.

Fig. 75. The dagger found on the body shown in Fig. 74.

Fig. 76. Scarab of the 'deputy treasurer' Aamu and a vessel found in his tomb.

Another group of foreign people living in Egypt in the Second Intermediate Period were the Nubians. Unlike the Palestinian settlers, they probably came to serve as soldiers under the Egyptians, and most had rather simple 'pan-grave' burials in accordance with their relatively low status. These graves are normally shallow and round; the body was laid in them in a contracted position. Pottery and sometimes weapons are placed in the burial; whereas earlier graves contained almost exclusively Nubian objects, later ones show signs that these people were becoming Egyptianised, as several Egyptian objects were found there.

The Second Intermediate Period was a difficult age for Egypt in terms of political history. Political disunity clearly led to economic decline over much of the country. Most art and luxury objects of the period are of low quality. It seems that in this impoverished period there was no capacity to

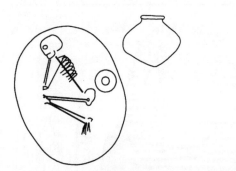

Fig. 77. Two pan-grave burials. Balabish tomb 223 (*left*); next to the body was a vessel. The buried person wore shells as personal adornments. Remains of leather and rope show that this individual may have been buried in everyday clothing. Qau 1307 (*right*) belongs to a young man. He was wrapped in linen and had shells as jewellery by his left wrist.

produce objects specially for burial on a large scale, and this holds true for the elite burials of the Egyptians as well. There are some exceptions, however. Coffins are clearly made only for tombs, and there are some canopic boxes (although they do not contain canopic jars) datable to the Second Intermediate Period. Finally there are many shabti figures dating roughly to this time, though they may belong to the very end of the period. They are mainly made of wood with rough hieroglyphic or more often hieratic inscriptions. The number of these surviving shabtis is relatively high, showing that they must have been popular. Sadly so far few have been found in a well documented undisturbed tombs, and their exact date therefore remains debatable.

In the Second Intermediate Period there are strong signs that burial customs changed radically. The anthropoid coffin became very popular and was now, especially in elite burials, the only coffin, although box coffins were still in use. The commonest anthropoid coffin is the 'rishi' coffin, showing the deceased with a nemes head-dress and a feather pattern covering the whole body (rishi means 'feathered' in Arabic). Tombs were now filled with objects from daily life, such as furniture, baskets and pottery. Evidently even in elite burials such objects replaced products of the funerary industry which still existed in the early Thirteenth Dynasty; sadly only a few have survived to pinpoint stages in this development.

There are big gaps in our knowledge of the development of Egyptian burial in the Second Intermediate Period. One reason is that most tombs of kings and related tombs of high officials have not yet been found and excavated. Nevertheless, a few important burials are known from Thebes, and others from Abydos, which was still a major centre. At the beginning of the nineteenth century the Italian excavator Guiseppe Passalacqua discovered the burial of queen Mentuhotep, wife of the Seventeenth Dynasty king Djehuty. Her mummified body was found in an anthropoid coffin inside a box-shaped one inscribed with an early version of the 'Book of the Dead'. The coffin had not been removed from the tomb when found

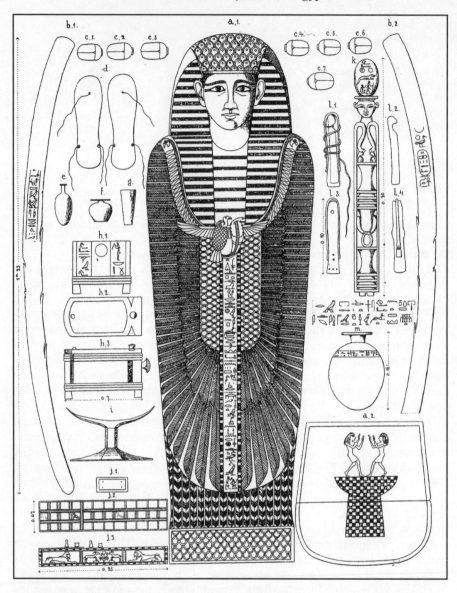

Fig. 78. The tomb group of Hornakht (end of the Seventeenth Dynasty – reading of name following S. Quirke), found at Thebes. Hornakht was placed in a rishi coffin. Many objects of daily use (in this case maybe better termed 'luxury objects') were found next to the coffin. There is a game board (*below left*), sandals, a head-rest and throwsticks. Some of these items are re-used or heirlooms. One calcite vessel (*centre right*) is from the Old Kingdom.

and its inscriptions and decoration were later copied by John Gardner Wilkinson. Other objects from the tomb include a canopic box without jars, a reed box with some vessels and maybe a silver funerary diadem.[14] Nothing was known until very recently about the burials of court officials in the Seventeenth Dynasty. The year 2000 saw the discovery of the tomb of the 'treasurer' Teti, an important official at the royal court under king Nubkheperre Intef. His small tomb chapel was found next to the pyramid of the king and was adorned with paintings. No information is yet available concerning its shaft and burial chamber.[15]

Very few undisturbed Seventeenth Dynasty tombs are known. One is a burial that Flinders Petrie excavated in 1908/09 at Thebes. It was simply placed in a hole in the desert, far from other burials – the distance doubtless helped to keep it intact. The tomb contained the body of a woman in her late teens or early twenties, wrapped in linen in a partly gilded coffin. The mummy was adorned with fine jewellery: a gold collar, bangles, an expertly cut scarab, earrings and an electrum girdle with several pieces in the form of shells. The coffin itself is a typical rishi coffin. Sadly most of the inscriptions have faded and the name of the woman remains unknown. The burial goods were placed around the coffin. On the left side of the coffin was a wooden stick. On this ten nets had been arranged, containing a variety of pottery vessels. Most of the latter are types in daily use, but there are also some Nubian pots (most likely imports) and some calcite vessels. A wonderful anhydrite bowl found in a basket may be of Middle Kingdom date. At the foot end of the coffin were a box containing some kind of ointment, a large pad of linen, two flat stools and a broken chair. Next to the objects were some items of food, including loaves of bread and fruits. Another big box found at the foot end contained the burial of a two- to three-year-old child. The two coffins are the only objects in the tomb made specially for burial. All other burial goods seem to be everyday objects (see Fig. 78 for a similar tomb group).[16]

6. The New Kingdom:
Death in an Affluent Society

The kings of the New Kingdom created a vast empire, conquering parts of Nubia and the Near East. Enormous quantities of raw materials and treasure were brought to Egypt, and this wealth is well reflected in the burial goods of the time. Tombs are more richly equipped than ever before or after. In its burial customs the New Kingdom can be divided into two main periods, with several subdivisions.

The early New Kingdom closely follows the customs of the Second Intermediate Period. Objects from daily life are still very common, with only a few items, such as the coffin or shabtis, being specially produced for burial. However, it is often hard to determine which objects belong to which category – domestic, religious, or exclusively funerary. To take just one example, a special type of pottery found in Eighteenth Dynasty tombs, a small angular bowl with a narrow foot, is very typical of burials. It is so common in graves of the period that it seems to be not so much a domestic object as perhaps a container for special food offerings as part of a funerary ritual. However, the vessel itself may have been used in daily life as tableware; the special context of the funeral turns it into a religious object.[1] Under Hatshepsut/Thutmosis III some essential changes are visible in the world of the tomb, such as the introduction of a new coffin type and the introduction of funerary papyri. Objects produced for burial become very important in elite tombs. The reign of Amenhotep III saw the introduction of further new classes of objects, e.g. a special type of shabti and anthropoid sarcophagi of hard stone. The burial customs of the brief Amarna period are still a mystery, but burials in the decades that follow seem in many respects very similar to those of the reign of Amenhotep III. The tombs were filled with objects from daily life; elite burials had in addition many items specially made for the tomb.

The big change in burial customs comes under Ramses II, when all objects from daily life disappear from tombs. All objects placed there are now specially produced for burial: coffins, shabtis, funerary papyri and amulets, to name just the most important. Poor people, unable to afford such products, had no burial goods. In terms of burial customs the Ramesside period is therefore totally different from the early New Kingdom and closer to the Third Intermediate and Late Period, when the same categories of objects were placed in tombs.

6. The New Kingdom: Death in an Affluent Society

The Eighteenth Dynasty before Amenhotep III

As already mentioned, burial equipment at the beginning of the Eighteenth Dynasty is almost identical to that of the Seventeenth. Many objects from daily life, such as furniture and several kinds of clothing, form an important part of elite tomb goods. Alongside these simple household goods there are some items made for burial which are very typical of the time. The coffins of elite burials are most often anthropoid, although at the beginning of the Eighteenth Dynasty box-shaped examples are still very common. Anthropoid coffins which follow the shape of the mummy were usually painted white with vertical bands of inscription. Coffins of the early Eighteenth Dynasty often bear scenes showing the dead or a funerary procession. In the early Eighteenth Dynasty a standard inscription developed which appeared on almost all the inscribed private coffins of the New Kingdom. On the box are shown the four children of Horus, and sometimes Thot and Anubis. The figures are accompanied with special texts which are also part of 'Book of the Dead' spell 151. Under Hatshepsut 'white coffins' were replaced by 'black coffins' (yellow or golden inscriptions on a black background).

The most famous feature of burial developed around this time is the so-called 'Book of the Dead'. In the late Middle Kingdom it was no longer common to place funerary literature in the burial chamber; there are only a few coffins of the period with religious texts. However, at the end of the Seventeenth Dynasty funerary texts in tombs again became popular, but written on linen shrouds, not on the coffin. The coffins of this time were anthropoid; this shape was not very suitable for long texts,[2] which may partly explain why religious literature was written on shrouds instead. From the end of the Middle Kingdom the corpus of funerary writings had continued to evolve. This development is hard to follow as not many religious writings of the Second Intermediate Period have survived. Many texts on the shrouds are entirely unknown from earlier periods, while others represent new versions of the coffin texts of the Middle Kingdom. In essence, coffin texts and the 'Book of the Dead' are simply earlier and later phases of a single continuing tradition of burial texts. Shrouds did not remain common manuscript material for long: textiles are not a very good writing substrate. By the first half of the Eighteenth Dynasty (under Hatshepsut) religious texts were being written on the normal Egyptian material for written texts, papyrus paper, with these scrolls being placed close to the mummy in many elite tombs. It is important to remember that not all elite tombs contained a 'Book of the Dead', and that some compositions were written on other objects in the burial, including the shabti, as we shall see below.

Other new burial goods under Hatshepsut/Thutmosis III include 'heart scarabs'. These had appeared sporadically in the Thirteenth Dynasty, but are common only from the Eighteenth Dynasty onwards. The flat underside of these scarabs was inscribed with 'Book of the Dead' chapter

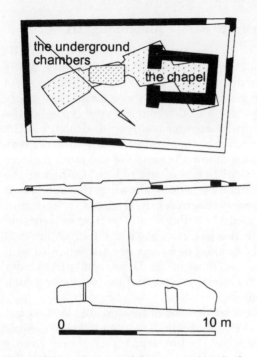

Fig. 79. Plan and section of the excavated tomb of a king's son called Teti. The chapel is only very poorly preserved, with just small fragments of the painted decoration. The mouth of the shaft which leads to the three underground burial chambers is just in front of the entrance to the chapel.

30. The scarab did not replace the heart of the deceased, as is sometimes assumed, but was specially made to protect it and was placed on the chest of the mummy.[3] Some tombs also contained four so-called 'magical bricks'. These are a set of mud-bricks inscribed with a short text and normally placed at the four sides of the burial chamber, but there are also examples where the bricks are arranged in pairs in niches on facing walls. On each brick an amulet was placed: a djed-pillar, a jackal, a torch and a shabti-like figure. These texts and images also appear in some 'Books of the Dead' (chapter 151). In the middle of the Eighteenth Dynasty other new object types in elite tombs included models of objects from daily life, particularly stone vessels and scribal palettes. Shabtis now appear more often in small numbers in elite burials, but are not common in tombs of less well-to-do people. The mummification process was further refined; organs and the brain were removed from the body, which was then dried out in natron, filled with molten resin and packed with linen. The most accomplished examples of embalming belong to the New Kingdom and the Third Intermediate Period.

There is little information about the tombs of high officials at Thebes, the court necropolis, in the early Eighteenth Dynasty, but the standard version seems to have included a free-standing chapel, built of mud-brick and decorated on the inside with paintings (Figs 79-80). Some of these chapels have been excavated, but there must have been many more of these vulnerable structures, now either totally destroyed or not yet found. The burial chambers were reached by a shaft situated next to the chapel.[4] Little can be said about the funerary equipment as all of these tombs have been heavily looted. The decoration of the tomb chapel seems to include scenes of the burial procession[5] and of the tomb owner and his family.[6] Many of these tombs may have had a stela in the chapel.

The main known burial type at Thebes for a high-ranking courtier in the middle of Eighteenth Dynasty is the rock-cut tomb (Fig. 81). Hundreds of tomb chapels were cut into the rock on the west bank there. Most were decorated with paintings or in some cases with reliefs. These decorated parts were freely accessible to the living. By contrast, the burial chamber was closed, located at the bottom of a

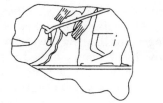

Fig. 80. These and similar fragments of paintings were found in Teti's chapel, showing that it was once decorated with very fine paintings.

shaft carved deep into the rock and rarely decorated. This tomb type already appears sporadically in the early Eighteenth Dynasty, but becomes common under Hatshepsut.

People of lower status also had brick chapels, although again little has been preserved. Most such tombs found so far have been looted, so we know little about the funerary goods. Fortunately, some tombs of lower-ranking people do survive, offering an impression of typical tomb equipment. The tomb of Ramose and Hatnefer, parents of the famous Senenmut, the most important official of Hatshepsut, was found undisturbed. The burial was discovered in a rough rock-cut chamber in Thebes West, not far from the tomb of their son, and contained several coffins. There were two anthropoid ones, one for Ramose (Senenmut's father) and the other for Hatnefer (his mother). Hatnefer's belongs to the 'black coffin' type and is partly covered with gold leaf. Ramose's is by comparison rather simple, and belongs to the 'white coffin' type that was very common in the early Eighteenth Dynasty.[7] Next to the anthropoid coffins of Hatnefer and Ramose two simple box coffins were found, both undecorated. One

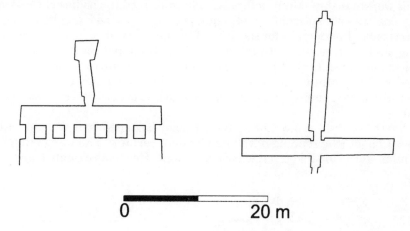

0   20 m

Fig. 81. Thebes, two New Kingdom rock-cut tomb chapels, of Ineni (*left*), a re-used Middle Kingdom chapel; and of the 'high priest of Amun' Ahmes (*right*). Most Theban chapels follow this T-shape plan.

contained two women and two children; the other a woman and a child. The mummy of Hatnefer was packed with eighteen shawls and sheets of linen; including a pair bearing the throne name (Maatkare) of Hatshepsut. A shroud at the head was inscribed with 'Book of the Dead' chapters 72 and 17. A gilt mask was placed over Hatnefer's head. On the breast of the mummy was found a bundle of funerary manuscripts – two papyri and a leather roll; the leather roll bearing 'Book of the Dead' chapter 100, often a separate charm. On the mummy the heart scarab and a small mirror were also found, at its left hand a set of rings and scarabs. The other objects of daily life found in the tomb probably also belonged to Hatnefer. There is no real proof of this as they are not inscribed, but Hatnefer is the person with the most elaborate coffin, indicating that she was the owner of most of the objects. These other finds include seven baskets containing food, linen and embalming material, three boxes with linen, three calcite jars, seven pottery jars and six pottery dishes. More important are a canopic box (containing the canopic jars, one of them with a jackal head, the others with human heads), a razor, a pair of sandals, a kohl jar and stick, a pillow, a set of silver vessels, and a bead necklace.[8]

Similar multiple burials from the Eighteenth Dynasty have been found in many parts of Egypt. A well preserved example is the tomb of Maket at Lahun, a town next to the pyramid of Senusret II at the entrance to the Fayum. At the end of the Thirteenth Dynasty the settlement was abandoned, and in the Eighteenth Dynasty an empty cellar in one of the houses was enlarged and used as a burial chamber. About fourteen coffins were found, most placed in two layers. Each contained several bodies, sometimes up to five or six. Most were simple, undecorated boxes; only one was decorated at the short ends with pictures of Isis and Nephthys. Two others were anthropoid, but are described by the excavator as of rather poor workmanship. Many coffins simply contained the bodies of the dead, but one was exceptionally well equipped. It contained a golden scarab inscribed in hieroglyphs for the 'lady of the house, Maket', a silver and gold ring, and a silver ring with the name of the same person (Fig. 82). Other objects found in the coffin are earrings, a bronze mirror, a kohl stick, a reed which contained musical reed pipes (Fig. 83), a head-rest (without picture), a vase imported from Cyprus and one other pottery vessel (Fig. 84).[9]

Farther south, tomb 183 at Beni Hasan belonged to a woman called Dedet-baqet (the reading of the name is not certain). She was perhaps of similar status to Maket, but was buried alone. Her tomb chamber was very

Fig. 82. Jewellery found in Maket's coffin; (*right*) one of the two earrings found.

small and contained an uninscribed wooden coffin. Next to it were found a small table, a large basket containing the legs and seat of a chair, a wooden head-rest, a large reed mat, a leather gourd and a well preserved drum. Inside the coffin the excavator, John Garstang, found an arrow case containing arrows and a broken bow. The head of the mummy was covered by a mummy mask. Beside these objects were some fragments of wooden models. The date of the tomb remains problematic. Pottery would be the best guide, but no illustration has been published of the only pot from this burial. The fragments of the wooden models point to a date in the

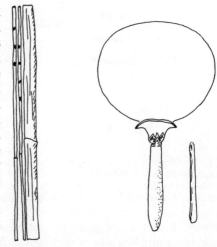

Fig. 83. Three reed musical instruments, a bronze mirror and a kohl stick from Maket's coffin.

Twelfth Dynasty, but all the other finds suggest a later date, perhaps in the early New Kingdom. All items apart from the coffin and the mummy mask are everyday objects typical of the late Seventeenth and early Eighteenth Dynasties. If we accept a New Kingdom date then the tomb may have been re-used, with the wooden models remnants of an original Middle Kingdom burial.[10]

At Harageh, not far from Lahun, a small New Kingdom cemetery was excavated. The tombs found are in general rather poor and illustrate the burial customs of ordinary farmers at that time. In most cases, the bodies were placed in holes in the ground, though some people were buried in a simple shaft or in a shaft tomb with one or two chambers. Many have been very heavily looted, but there are a few tombs for which more detailed information is available. Tomb 273 is a Middle Kingdom shaft tomb with two chambers, re-used in the New Kingdom to hold the remains of five men and eight women. The few funerary goods comprise four pottery jars, some beads and two scarabs, one with the name of Amenhotep I (Fig. 85). Wooden fragments may be those of coffins. Tomb 363 – a simple shaft – contained the remains of seven women and six men. Burial goods include many 'mud' pots, eight pottery vessels, a bronze pin, some beads, a stone vessel, a scarab and a ring bearing the name of Thutmosis IV.[11]

Fig. 84. Pottery found in the Maket's coffin. The vessel on the left is an import from Cyprus.

There is equally limited information about the burial customs of the common people at Thebes. Petrie excavated such a tomb in 1896, consisting of two chambers, one upper and one

Fig. 85. Object found in Harageh tomb 273. The published excavation report gives only the types found (e.g. just one bead was published from a string of identical beads). It is possible that for some of the pottery types several pots were found. The scarab gives the name of Amenhotep I; a second scarab found in the tomb was not published.

lower, which could each be entered through a separate corridor. Both corridors and chambers were found full of mummies, as Petrie describes: 'the upper passage and chamber was closely filled with at least two layers of bodies, over eighty being packed into it. .... These bodies can scarcely be called mummies, as they seem to have been buried in wrappings without any attempts at preserving the flesh by resin, oil, or salts. Hence there was only a confused mass of bones amid a deep soft heap of brown dust.'[12] The tomb had been plundered, and the only finds were numerous pottery vessels. The burial was relatively well dated as it was found under the mortuary temple of king Thutmosis IV, and must therefore be earlier.

Beside the mass and multiple burials there are still many people buried in simple tombs without chamber or shaft (see Figs 86, 87). It is hard to decide to which social level these people belong. Multiple burials may often represent family tombs; they do not necessarily belong to the poorest, who would not have had the resources for a rock-cut chamber of the required size. The poor would therefore have been buried mostly in single tombs, although a multiple burial might well have contained richer and poorer members of the same family. Multiple burials such as the tomb of Maket contain valuable objects showing the small wealth of at least some of the people buried here.

Up to this point all the burials we have discussed have been isolated examples from across Egypt. For comparison, it is worth examining one

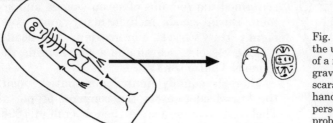

Fig. 86. Qau tomb 490: the undisturbed tomb of a man. The only grave good was a scarab found at the left hand. The buried person was in all probability of quite low status.

72

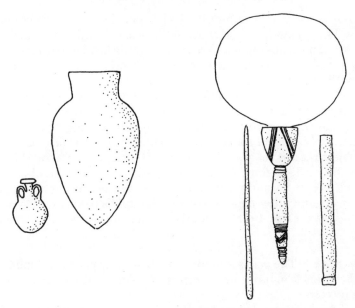

Fig. 87. Gurob tomb O1: objects found in the burial of a woman (?). The body was covered with a closely woven mat of grass and was wrapped in another mat made from date palm ribs. The body itself was mummified. The two vessels (*left*) were found at the head end of the burial. The cosmetic objects (mirror, long narrow kohl pot, kohl stick – *right*) were found on the chest. Burials with the bodies wrapped in a reed mat clearly belong to the poorest levels of society and are found in almost all periods and regions of Egypt.

well documented case of an entire Eighteenth Dynasty cemetery. The best examples come from Lower Nubia, which was conquered and to some extent colonised by the Egyptians during the New Kingdom. Although it is unlikely that many Egyptians lived and were buried there, it is clear that the material culture of Lower Nubia became fully Egyptianised, though some local variants in pottery production may have existed. The burial customs may have been different in detail from those in Egypt, but this remains to be researched. The following burials can be taken as examples of local or provincial culture in the New Kingdom.

Lower Nubia is one of the best excavated regions in North Africa. In the early 1960s the Aswan High Dam was built. It was clear that once it came into use vast parts of Nubia would be permanently under water. For that reason UNESCO launched a campaign to save monuments and to excavate settlements and cemeteries in the area to be flooded. One of the rescue missions was the Scandinavian Joint Expedition, which excavated some extensive cemeteries. These have been published and are now a prime source for the burial customs in that region and for the New Kingdom.

One of the cemeteries lies near the modern village of Fadrus. About 680 burials were excavated. Some other tombs may have been lost or unable to be excavated since parts of the cemetery were covered with modern houses. With this in mind the burial ground is big enough to have served

73

a relatively dense rural community. It flourished mainly in the Eighteenth Dynasty. The excavators distinguished five social rankings, which we will follow here. These distinctions are made mainly according to the numbers of pottery vessels found in each tomb. The poorest (social rank 1) are the tombs without any finds (23% of the excavated tombs). Social rank 2 consists of burials with one to four pots (48.8% of the excavated tombs). The third rank contain four or more pots (20% of the excavated tombs). Together the three lowest social ranks make up more than 90% of the tombs found. Burials of social rank 4 include both four or more pots, and metal objects, such as weapons or metal vessels (1.8% of the tombs). Finally the richest tombs are those with a burial chamber built in mud-brick. They normally contain several vessels, mummy masks and metal objects and other objects. 6.8% of the tombs belong to this category. Tombs of social rank 4 and 5 clearly belong to the social elite buried at Fadrus.

Social rank 1. The poorest tombs. The body was placed extended on the left, right or back in a not very deep shaft. There are no grave goods and there is no coffin.

Social rank 2. An example is tomb 185:73 (Fig. 88).[13] The tomb belongs to a mature man who was buried in a shaft. The burial goods consist of three stone vessels and some pottery vessels arranged at the head and at the feet of the dead.

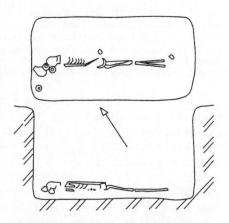

Social rank 3. An example of this social group is 185:331.[14] The burial was placed in a fairly shallow shaft tomb in a chamber to the east. The body was laid in an anthropoid wooden coffin, which may have been plastered and painted. There were some beads found around the neck. The only other finds are five different pottery vessels arranged around the coffin.

Fig. 88. Tomb 185:75 near Fadrus (Nubia). The tomb is a simple shallow shaft.

Social rank 4. An example is tomb 185:196, quite a wealthy burial arranged in a shallow shaft with a side-chamber (Fig. 89).[15] The side-chamber was once closed with a brick wall. The dead person, an adult, was lying on its back, hands at its sides. The head was covered with a partly gilt stucco mask. At the neck were a scarab-like seal mounted in gold and a gold pendant. Around the body, especially at the head, at the feet and left of the head/chest were many pottery vessels. The latter clearly belong to the funerary meal. On the left side of the legs was a bronze axe. Nothing is really known about the person buried here; it is not even

Fig. 89. Fadrus tomb 185:196. The burial
chamber is 3.3 m long.

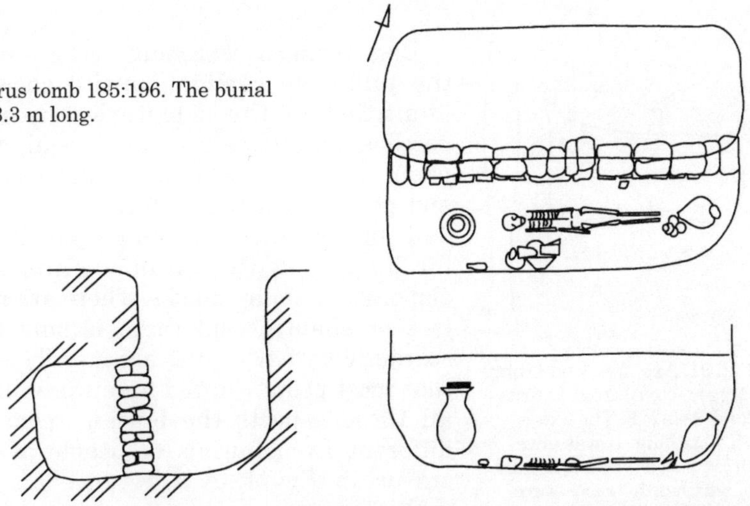

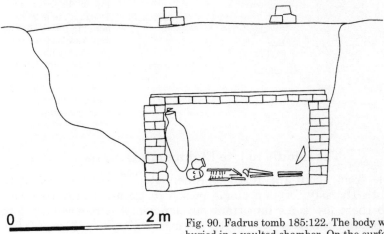

possible to say if it was a man or a women. No object bears an inscription,
but the few gold items demonstrate the relative wealth of the tomb owner.

Social rank 5. An example is tomb 185:122, one of the richer burials at
Fadrus (Fig. 90). The body was placed in a vaulted brick chamber with a
coated floor, which was additionally coated with a layer of clay. The head
was covered with a stucco mask, while next to the legs were a bronze axe
and a dagger (Fig. 91). A box must also have stood at the head, since metal
fittings were found there. Concentrated at the head and at the feet were
several pottery vessels. At the 'head end' of the chamber was finally a huge
storage jar (Fig. 92). There were traces of a superstructure over the burial
chamber which must have belonged to some kind of chapel.[16]

0   2 m

Fig. 90. Fadrus tomb 185:122. The body was
buried in a vaulted chamber. On the surface
above the tomb was a mud-brick structure which
once belonged to a chapel or even a small pyramid.

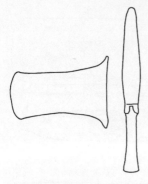

Fig. 91. Axe *(left)* and bronze dagger *(right)* from Fadrus tomb 185:122. The axe is 13.7 cm long. It was once fitted into a wooden handle, of which only traces were found. The dagger is 27.5 cm long. The presence of weapons in the tomb may indicate that a man was buried here.

Despite imperfect conditions for preservation, the following common burial goods can be identified in the cemeteries near Fadrus: personal adornments, cosmetic equipment (kohl pots), weapons, tools, stone and metal vessels and pottery. All these objects are also used in daily life, but there are items specially produced for burials, with several coffins and some elaborate mummy masks. There are no canopic jars or shabtis, and there is only one heart scarab. Very few objects are inscribed, implying that most people buried here were illiterate. In all these aspects the burials seem not very different from burials of people of the same status in Egypt. A difference may be that multiple burials are not so common as in Egypt, and that even the richest tombs are without inscriptions, but this might be just an accident of the surviving record.

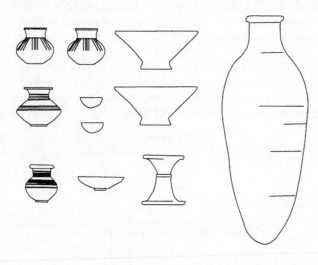

Fig. 92. Fadrus tomb 185:122: the pottery found in the tomb. The two vessels in the top centre may have contained gifts for the tomb owner. The large storage jar on the right was probably for drinking water.

The middle to late Eighteenth Dynasty

The time from about the reign of Amenhotep III to the end of the Eighteenth Dynasty forms a single period in terms of burial customs, although there are some important developments. A particularly large number of undisturbed or only partly disturbed elite burials survive from the Eighteenth Dynasty. The most famous of these is the tomb of Tuya and Yuya, parents of queen Teye (wife of king Amenhotep III). The tomb was found in the Valley of the Kings and is only partly disturbed.[17] An entirely intact find from the same reign is the tomb of the 'overseer of works' Kha and his wife Meryt, also in Thebes.[18] The tomb of the 'royal fan bearer' Maiherperi, only partly disturbed, was again found in the Valley of the Kings and may date to the reign of Amenhotep II. There is also the burial of a certain Hatiay together with a woman called Henutwedjebu and the ladies Siamen and Huy.[19] These tombs contain several kinds of objects already discussed or mentioned for other Eighteenth Dynasty tombs. Many items found in these high status burials are artworks of the highest quality. The overwhelming bulk of their funerary equipment consists of objects from daily life: vessels, furniture, cosmetic objects and even chariots, proving the extent to which the custom of putting into tombs objects formerly used in the house was followed, especially at this high social level. Another focal point of the burial was the coffin. Anthropoid coffins were most common in the Eighteenth Dynasty. The tombs of some of the high status people mentioned contained a partly gilded outer box coffin, in which anthropoid coffins were placed. Other important parts of the funerary equipment were the four canopic jars in the canopic box, some shabtis and a papyrus text of the 'Book of the Dead'. Other mummiform figures look like shabtis, but do not bear the shabti text and may have a different function. Dummy or model objects, especially wooden vases, plastered and painted to imitate stone vessels and dummy scribal palettes ('cheaper' copies of objects from daily life) are also well attested.

The reign of Amenhotep III saw some special developments in funerary practice. For the first time anthropoid sarcophagi (stone coffins) are attested. Box-shaped examples are very common in elite burials from the Old and Middle Kingdom, but for the early Eighteenth Dynasty, before Amenhotep III, nothing of the kind is securely attested. There may be several reasons for this. One is perhaps the shape of coffins. The sarcophagi of the Old and Middle Kingdom copied common wooden box coffins. In the New Kingdom the anthropoid form of coffin became common, but always made in wood. To cut an anthropoid sarcophagus must have been very expensive and needed more specialised stone cutters than were required for the production of a simple stone box. The few sarcophagi of the early Eighteenth Dynasty are again in shape of a box (they belong to the kings of the period and to the officials Senenmut and the 'viceroy of Kush' Nehesi – both very important persons). Under Amenhotep III the first anthropoid sarcophagi are attested. The 'viceroy of Kush' Merymose – again a very powerful figure at court – had a set of three sarcophagi, copies in superbly executed granodiorite and red granite of the contemporary 'black coffins'. Another very important person of that time is Amenhotep, son of Hapu, who was in later times worshipped as a god. Amenhotep had a set of two sarcophagi, an outer box-shaped one and an inner anthropoid one. Sadly all these were smashed in remote antiquity. Isolated fragments exist in several collections all over the world.

Wooden coffins from the reign of Amenhotep III also display certain innovations. The outer coffin of Yuya, father-in-law of the king, is of the normal 'black type'. However, the four children of Horus, formerly almost always depicted with human heads, now each have a different head (falcon, jackal, baboon, human), as was to become the norm in the Nineteenth Dynasty. Yuya's middle coffins have a picture of Nut on the cover, and Yuya holds in his hands a djed and a tiyet amulet. Both

Fig. 93. Shabti of Merymery from Saqqara.

symbols are again typical of later coffins and appear here for the first time in this position. Another new object type is the shabti box. In the late Middle Kingdom shabtis were often placed in model coffins or model (box) sarcophagi. Under Amenhotep III small shrine-shaped boxes, in which a shabti was placed, are attested for the first time.[20] At the end of the dynasty these boxes became double-vaulted shrines and were used for many shabtis. The shabti boxes are very typical of Thebes and found only sporadically in other cemeteries, where pottery vessels (sometimes painted) containing shabtis are more common. Another innovation under Amenhotep III, but one that is not often attested later, are small statues in limestone showing the tomb owner performing several tasks. These statues recall the servant figures found in Old Kingdom tombs and it seems possible that they copied these figures. However, the figures produced under Amenhotep III show the tomb owner and are therefore more similar to the shabtis (Fig. 93).

Under Amenhotep III Saqqara, the cemetery of Memphis, became an important burial ground for high officials. The city must have been the administrative centre of Egypt throughout the Eighteenth Dynasty. Presumably because the king was buried at Thebes, all high courtiers were at first also buried there. Under Amenhotep III, however, many of them decided to build their tombs at Saqqara. The most famous so far discovered is that of the northern vizier Aperel; other burials are those of the 'treasurer' Meryre, the 'high steward' Amenhotep, and members of the family of the vizier Ptahmose.

Almost nothing is known about the burial customs of the Amarna period. The few objects from tombs datable to the period give the impression that only the inscriptions changed (Osiris is not mentioned any more). Funerary beliefs may have been totally different, but the objects placed in the tomb are identical with those found in earlier burials. There are many shabtis datable to the period, though with a different formula.[21]

78

In the royal tomb fragments of a canopic chest were found, while in a tomb in the Valley of the Kings (KV 55) datable to the end of the Amarna period, four canopic jars and four magical bricks were discovered. There are some coffins datable to the period, and these have a slightly different design. The coffin of a woman called Ta-aat has the normal mummy shape, but the scenes on the coffin show the deceased at the offering table or together with the family, instead of the four children of Horus and Anubis. The texts mention Aton and Akhet-Aton (the ancient name of Amarna). Fragments of a similar decorated sarcophagus, and a model coffin from Amarna with such scenes are also known. Both certainly belong to the Amarna period.[22] The decoration in the tombs of the court officials at Amarna focuses on scenes of the king adoring the sun. The tomb owner himself becomes secondary. Similar scenes – although the tomb owner is always very important – were found in the tombs of high officials under Amenhotep III.[23]

Shortly after the Amarna period a new coffin type developed, showing the deceased on the lid clothed as in daily life (see Fig. 108). This type is first attested on sarcophagi at Saqqara, but became popular throughout the country in the early Nineteenth Dynasty. The best preserved examples are all from Thebes. In the post-Amarna period Saqqara finally became the most important court cemetery. Only people working in the south (the southern vizier, the 'viceroy of Kush', the Amun temple staff) were still buried at Thebes. The main tomb type at Saqqara was a temple-like structure, although there are also some rock-cut tombs. The bigger of these tombs consist of several columned courtyards and three chapels at the back with a stela as the main cult object (while in Thebes the main cult objects were statues). The walls of these buildings were decorated with reliefs showing scenes of daily life, mainly in connection with the office of the tomb owner and funerary processions. The chapels at the back of such tombs are often decorated with scenes from the 'Book of the Dead'. These tombs vary greatly in size. The larger ones are on the scale of a medium-sized temple. The least imposing often consist of only a small chamber decorated with reliefs. The burial apartments are reached by a shaft, and are sometimes quite elaborately decorated. Those of the 'overseer of the treasury' Maya were paved with limestone slabs, decorated in sunk relief.[24] Not much has survived of the burial goods once placed in these tombs, but the few remains show that they were not very different from the objects placed in tombs under Amenhotep III. Remnants of elaborate furniture were found in the tomb of Maya.

The contents of the tomb of king Tutanhkamun need not be described in detail here. However, his whole burial equipment, with the high number of everyday objects, falls within the same tradition as the private burials described above, even if there are several objects of types reserved for royal burials. A series of wooden gilt statues, showing the king and several gods, were found in special shrines. Fragments of almost identical statues have been found in some other New Kingdom royal tombs, from Thutmosis III

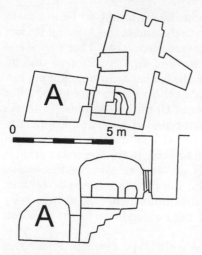

to the Ramesside period.[25] Many amulet types found on the mummy are attested here for the first time and appear hundreds of years later in private contexts. Other objects exclusive to royal burials are two 'guardian statues' showing the king in larger than life size, and the 'Osiris bed', which is almost only attested in royal burials in the New Kingdom. The 'Osiris bed' is a wooden board in the shape of an Osiris figure. On the board was earth and grain. The grain started to grow in the burial chamber or during a ritual, an impressive symbol of fertility. It is often hard to say if other objects had a special function in connection with the dead king. Is a 'throne' an 'object of daily use' or was it placed into the tomb for some special religious reason? Only signs of wear might tell.

Fig. 94. The tomb of Sennefer (A) was the side-chamber of a bigger tomb of a man called Hormes. The burial of Hormes was already plundered when the excavators found it. The door to the chamber of Sennefer was found intact. The burial is datable to shortly after the Amarna period.

The tomb of the 'servant in the place of truth' Sennefer and his wife Nefertiti was found in 1928 at Deir el-Medineh in a small chamber. The tomb may have been lightly robbed on one occasion, but still contained substantial parts of its equipment.[26] It will be presented here as an example of a New Kingdom elite burial. The mummies of Sennefer and Nefertiti were each placed in a black coffin, decorated with yellow inscriptions. The 'black coffin type' was still used in the late Eighteenth Dynasty, although other types such as yellow coffins (coffins with yellow background and colourful vignettes), coffins showing the dead in everyday dress, and sarcophagi were more popular for elite burials. A painted shroud lay on Sennefer's coffin, showing him in front of an offering table (Fig. 95). On his mummy was a gilt mask (Fig. 96), while Nefertiti's mummy had no mask, but was

Fig. 95. Over Sennefer's coffin was a pall on which this painted textile was found, showing Sennefer in front of an offering table.

Fig. 96. Sennefer's mummy mask.

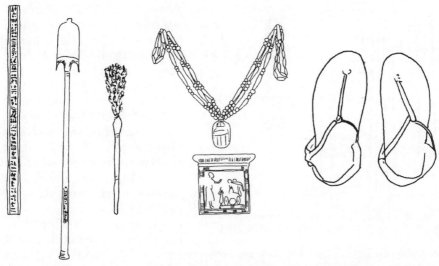

Fig. 97. Sennefer's burial yielded an abundant variety of flowers, but also contained other objects: (*left to right*) five inscribed wooden boards (only one is depicted); one fan; four staves with flowers of different sizes (only one is depicted); a heart scarab and a pectoral, both found on the mummy; and a pair of shoes found in a box.

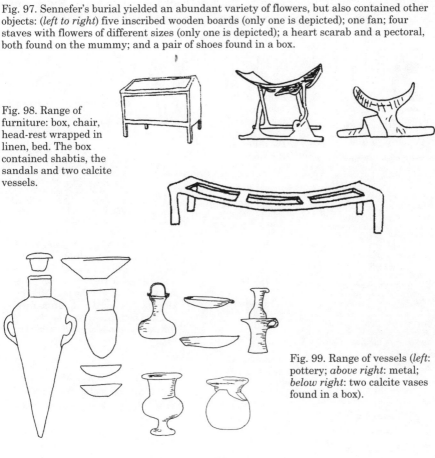

Fig. 98. Range of furniture: box, chair, head-rest wrapped in linen, bed. The box contained shabtis, the sandals and two calcite vessels.

Fig. 99. Range of vessels (*left*: pottery; *above right*: metal; *below right*: two calcite vases found in a box).

Fig. 100. Coffin of the child from Sennefer's burial, a shabti and a second shabti wrapped in linen.

adorned with an array of jewellery, notably two rings, one in silver and the other in electrum (gold-silver). A small box in the tomb contained the mummy of a child (Fig. 100). Both coffins were surrounded by furniture, such as a bed and boxes, containing various objects. There were two shabtis in another box, both wrapped in linen, and closely datable to the post-Amarna period by their style.

An example of poorer interment, although it is not possible to determine the precise social status, is the burial of a young woman and a child belonging to the late Eighteenth or early Nineteenth Dynasty, found at Saqqara near the Teti pyramid (Figs 101-106).[27] They

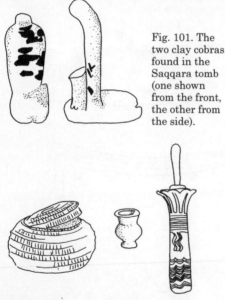

Fig. 101. The two clay cobras found in the Saqqara tomb (one shown from the front, the other from the side).

Fig. 102. Amulets and beads found in the burial of the child. Some of the figures (Bes, Taweret, the magical head) are well known from the ivory wands of the late Middle Kingdom. Magical wands and these amulets had the same function: protection of mother and child at birth.

Fig. 103. A basket, a stone vessel and a glass kohl-pot.

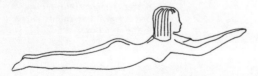

Fig. 104. A cosmetic spoon in the shape of a swimming naked lady.

lay together inside a badly decayed coffin. Next to the woman's head had been placed three dom-palm fruits. At the northern end of the coffin were a round lidded basket with a small jug and a glass vessel in the shape of a palm column inside; a second basket with a calcite jar; several beads; a terracotta figure of a naked girl on a bed; two pottery figures of cobras; and a wooden head-rest. At the southern end of the coffin were found a pottery jar and a wooden spoon of a swimming girl.[28] The

Fig. 105. Further objects found in the burial: clay figure of a naked woman lying on a bed, a wedjat-eye, two balls (?) and a stone cup.

burial is of special interest for several reasons. The combination of a woman and an infant in one coffin very strongly suggests the burial of a mother and child. This places some of the items from the tomb in a new light. Most of the finds can be described as cosmetic objects, while the terracotta figure of a woman on a bed refers to mother and child. The cobra figures are especially interesting, because such figures have also been found in

Fig. 106. The pottery found in the tomb.

domestic contexts, where they might have some magical function. They presumably had a similar function in the burial. All objects in this burial, except the coffin and maybe the amulets, are objects of daily use or magical objects normally used in daily life, but they also clearly relate to the sex of the buried person. The cosmetic objects found fit perfectly with a woman of some small wealth.

7. The Late New Kingdom: Reduction to Essentials

The Nineteenth and Twentieth Dynasties

In the Ramesside period (the Nineteenth and Twentieth Dynasties) new objects and object groups were introduced into elite burials. The four canopic jars now each had a different head: ape for Hapi, jackal for Duamutef, human for Amset and hawk for Qebehsenuef. The number of shabtis increased, with five to twenty or more not uncommon. They were often placed in a special box, which could be opened from the top and had room for two or three shabtis. Several of these boxes, which are usually brightly painted, are normally found in a single tomb. There are also the four magical bricks. Finally, a papyrus with the text of the 'Book of the Dead' is common. Several kinds of amulet, such as heart-shaped amulets with a human head, 'conventional' heart scarabs become important. Objects from daily life, such as furniture or pottery, seem to disappear slowly, although single examples of these types are still attested at some places. Almost all the objects placed in tombs are now made specially for burial (see Fig. 107).

In the Nineteenth Dynasty sarcophagi become common in the highest ranking burials (Fig. 108) – a list of the owners of sarcophagi of the Nineteenth Dynasty reads like a 'who's who' of the royal court at the time. These sarcophagi show the dead person with arms crossed over the chest, holding a tiyet and djed symbol. The space under the arms is decorated with bands of texts and vignettes (small scenes) carved in sunken relief into the stone. The material of these sarcophagi is often red granite, with relief decoration which was probably always painted, though unfortunately the colour has survived in only a few cases. In layout and shape the sarcophagi of the late Eighteenth Dynasty generally followed the development of contemporary wooden coffins, but in the Nineteenth Dynasty the two types of object seem to develop in different directions. The decoration of the stone sarcophagi is still similar to that of the wooden coffins, but they become broader in shape. There are some impressively well made pieces dating from the reign of Ramses II, but by the end of his reign most sarcophagi are quite clumsy, often with illegible inscriptions. At Saqqara one such sarcophagus was found containing a wooden board. There are no parallels, but it is possible that many of these sarcophagi once contained a better-made wooden coffin. The sarcophagus is now nothing more than a secondary container protecting both the body of the dead person and an elaborate decorated wooden coffin. Few sarcophagi can be

Fig. 107. Three faience pectorals from Riqqeh, Nineteenth or Twentieth Dynasty. Amulets and jewellery especially made for burial are very important in elite tombs of the Ramesside period.

dated to the Twentieth Dynasty and what examples there are were very badly made with only a few inscriptions. Sarcophagi for private people are no longer in common use.

At about the same time, scenes of daily life disappear from the chapels. Such scenes are still attested under Ramses II. The tomb chapel of Mose at Saqqara is famous for its long hieroglyphic inscription describing a court case involving a dispute over land. A scene in the tomb of the 'high priest of Amun' Nebwennef shows the priest in front of the king, who is standing at the 'window of appearance'. Tomb chapels of the later Nineteenth and Twentieth Dynasties are with few exceptions decorated exclusively with religious scenes, such as vignettes from the 'Book of the Dead', or scenes showing the tomb owner and his wife adoring different gods.

The archaeological record of burial customs in the Ramesside period is very different to that of the Eighteenth Dynasty. While there are many undisturbed tombs of high-ranking people from the Eighteenth Dynasty, there is almost nothing similar for the Nineteenth or Twentieth. The only exception is

Fig. 108. Sarcophagus lid, late Eighteenth or early Nineteenth Dynasty, showing the deceased in everyday dress.

85

the tomb of the 'servant of the place of truth' Sennedjem, which was found undisturbed in 1886. Multiple burials had become increasingly common, so it is not surprising that about twenty burials were found in Sennedjem's tomb. Many were not even placed in coffins, though the tomb owner and his son Khonsu had a set of two. Both had an outer box coffin, brightly painted with parts of the 'Book of the Dead'. Inside the outer coffin was a vividly painted 'yellow' coffin,[1] and within the latter a mummy board showing the dead person dressed as in daily life. The burials of these two men contained canopic boxes and shabti boxes filled with shabtis. Sennedjem was also provided with a mummy bed, a chair, a stool, some pottery vessels, staves and architectural instruments. The wives of the two men had a simpler set, with just one coffin and mummy board, again showing the women in daily dress, and some boxes for jewellery. The other people buried here are either placed in a simple coffin or have no coffin at all; at least some of them had shabtis.[2] The burial of Sennedjem took place under Sety I or in the first years of Ramses II. The exact date of the other burials is not known, but they may all have taken place within a short time-span, as all the objects are similar in style. The entrance of the burial chamber was closed by a wooden door, making it relatively easy to get in and place new burials in the tomb, at least for a while. The date when this door was closed forever is not known.

As already mentioned, no undisturbed elite burials of the Ramesside period are known. Disturbed burials therefore form our source for the objects placed in tombs at this time. The tomb of queen Nefertari is well-known for its beautiful paintings. It had been looted, but some objects were found in it. It was not re-used in the Late Period, in contrast to so many other New Kingdom tombs at Thebes, so all the items found must belong to the original equipment of the queen. The most important item is the largest object to have survived: the fragments of a huge box-shaped sarcophagus in red granite. There are also several wooden shabtis, most painted black with details and inscriptions in yellow. Two lids of boxes, one black and one decorated in bright colours, may belong to shabti boxes. Finally, there are some vessels and a pair of sandals. The most outstanding small object was a gilded djed-pillar with faience inlays which once formed part of a 'magical brick'. Other fragments of djed-pillars may have belong to boxes or other furniture. An interesting find is the knob of a chest bearing the name of the late Eighteenth Dynasty king Eje.[3] Most of these objects do not need much comment. However, the number of everyday objects is very small.

Nefersekheru, 'deputy of the treasury of the lord of the two lands', was an official of some standing, though not at the highest level at court. He was buried in a rock-cut tomb in Thebes, of which the relatively small tomb chapel, decorated with brightly painted scenes from the 'Book of the Dead', was quite well preserved. The underground chambers were reached by a sloping passage, typical of Ramesside tombs in Thebes and in marked contrast to tomb-shafts of the Eighteenth Dynasty before Amenhotep III.

In the burial apartments a few objects from the original equipment survived, although the whole tomb had been heavily looted and also later re-used. There is no coffin preserved for Nefersekheru, which makes it likely that he was not placed in a sarcophagus (which would have had a high chance of survival), but simply in a wooden coffin. Only small inscribed fragments of the canopic jars were found, while other parts of the original tomb equipment include rough clay shabtis and two fragments of a beautiful scribal palette, with long religious texts on it. A carnelian snakehead amulet bears the short inscription 'the Osiris Nefersekheru' (Fig. 109). Such amulets were common in the Ramesside

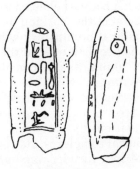

Fig. 109. Carnelian snake-head amulet from the tomb of Nefersekheru, bearing his name.

period and were worn around the neck. In the Middle Kingdom they were called 'menqebyt' or 'menqeryt' and may have had the function of supplying fresh air for the dead (it has also been suggested that they may have had something to do with protection against snakes). An important

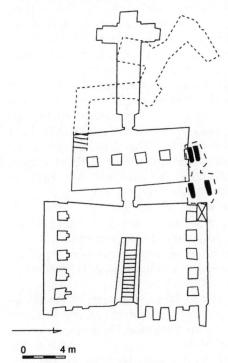

funerary object found in the tomb is the fragmentary funerary papyrus, on which Nefersekheru is shown together with his wife. Other objects include fragments of many pottery vessels, some baskets, and sandals. The latter recall the sandals from the tomb of queen Nefertari.[4]

The tomb of the 'high steward of Amun' Amenemope was also very much looted when found. Only a few objects of the original burial have survived. However, his high status is clear from his huge granite sarcophagus.[5] An important part of Amenemope's tomb complex was also a shaft in which four wooden coffins were found (Fig. 110). They are of the 'black coffin' type, but not of the highest quality; the inscriptions are often hard to read and some of the paintings are very poorly executed. Two of the coffins were produced as stock, with the place for the name of the coffin-owner left blank. One of the

0   4 m

Fig. 110. The tomb of Amenemope (Theban Tomb 41). The four coffins in the subsidiary tombs are in black.

other coffins belonged to the 'lady of the house' Huner and the fourth to the 'head of the working place of Amun' Nekhu-nefer. These burials are very likely contemporary with the tomb of Amenemope and it is possible that the people buried in the shaft belonged his entourage. The 'high steward of Amun' was responsible for the economic institutions of the temple of Amun, in which the 'working place of Amun' was clearly a key part.[6] Nekhu-nefer was therefore very likely on the staff of Amenemope. The bad preservation of many tombs and tomb equipment means that such close relationships between people working together are not often visible in burial complexes. However, there is another example at Saqqara, where a certain Iurudef was buried right next to his master the 'overseer of the treasury' Tia. Iurudef is depicted in Tia's tomb as his chief servant.[7]

As well as the disturbed burials excavated in Egypt, there are also some groups of objects in museums, which were found in undisturbed tombs in the nineteenth century. The problem with these is that it is only possible to assign items with the name of the owner to a particular burial. Uninscribed objects found in the same burial may be in the same museum, but it is not possible to assign them with any certainty to a particular group of burial objects. One example is the tomb equipment of the 'lady of the house' and 'chantress of Amun' Henutmehyt, now in the British Museum. From these titles and the quality of the funerary objects she belongs clearly to the highest social level. Henutmehyt had a set of two partly gilded anthropoid coffins. Inside them there was a mummy board in two parts: a mummy mask and an open-worked mummy board. Both objects are gilded. There was a simple undecorated canopic box with four wooden canopic jars in it, each with a differed shaped lid, as was common in the Ramesside Period. There are altogether forty shabtis and four brightly painted shabti boxes. The number of shabtis is exceptionally high and may indicate the high status of Henutmehyt. The burial included four magical bricks with their incised inscriptions and amulets. Finally there is a funerary papyrus of 'Book of the Dead' chapter 100, naming Henutmehyt. Women as owners of funerary papyri are not very common in the New Kingdom. They are normally shown together with their husbands on their papyri. There is also a box with mummified meat pieces. This box may belong to the burial, although this is uncertain as it is uninscribed. Only a description of the nineteenth-century discovery of the tomb would reveal whether other objects were buried with Henutmehyt; so far no reliable account is known.

Another trend in burial customs of the Ramesside period should be mentioned in connection with the tombs of the ruling elite. Most court officials of the early Eighteenth Dynasty are buried at Thebes, with only a few exceptions, such as the 'treasurer' Nehi, buried in Saqqara/Memphis during the reign of Hatshepsut. He is well known because he was very much involved in the Punt expedition. Under Amenhotep III, as we have seen, Saqqara became more popular with court elite officials, at least as burial place for the officials who worked and lived there (this was not always the case earlier on; there is even a 'mayor of Memphis' who had his tomb at Thebes). After the Amarna period Saqqara became a very popular burial place. Almost the whole court of Tutankhamun is buried there: the 'general' Haremhab, the 'overseer of the treasury' Maya, 'the high steward' Nia. Under Ramses II Saqqara is still very popular, but many high officials built their tombs in the provinces. The tombs of the 'vizier' Parahotep and his wife Huner,[8] and of the 'general' Paser were found at Sedment, the burial of the 'overseer of the treasury' Suti was excavated in Middle Egypt,[9] the 'overseer of the granary' Zaaset was laid to rest at Asyut,[10] while the tomb of a 'royal scribe of the lord of two lands' was discovered at El Mashayikh (near This).[11] The tomb of the 'high steward' Nefersekheru at Zawyet Sultan may be of slightly earlier date.[12] It is often hard to say why these officials were buried in these particular places, but the easiest explanation seems to be that they were born there.

It is possible to follow the changes of the burial customs in the Ramesside period better in relatively poor burials than in the looted tombs of the elite. Many well-recorded graves of the less wealthy come from Bubastis. Between 1968 and 1971 Ahmad El-Sawi excavated some 210 burials there, mainly of the New Kingdom. The most striking observation is the total lack of everyday objects; in particular, the excavators found almost no pottery. The absence of pottery complicates precise dating of the tombs, but the few finds in most cases point to the Ramesside period. Nevertheless it is hard to determine whether the few differences observed in the burials are variations current at one and the same time or whether they imply change over centuries.

In general there are only three types of burial goods: jewellery (including amulets), shabtis and coffins. Most common are amulets on the body, especially wedjat-eyes and scarabs, but also bead necklaces and armlets. In nine burials rough clay shabtis were found. They are normally placed inside pottery jars, positioned at the head or feet of the dead. The crude workmanship indicates that they do not belong to very rich people. The only other common burial good is the coffin. Most of the burials found were put in a rough pottery coffin or in a shaft, while children were often placed in a big jar. A pottery coffin in a pit is attested only once,[13] but there are some shafts with wooden coffins.[14] Finally, there were nine vaulted underground chambers which the excavator described as tombs. Some were used for several burials and may have been family tombs.

The evidence from the cemetery is that poorer people were placed in either pottery coffins or small shafts. The protection of the body was very important, as can be seen from the number of amulets; it is possible to interpret the shabtis in a similar way as helping the dead in the underworld. Anthropoid pottery coffins are typical for many not very rich burials; high quality examples copy contemporary wooden coffins in their decoration.[15] These pottery coffins are often also called slipper coffins, because the whole body of the coffin was formed like a tube; the body of the dead person must have been 'slipped' into it through the lidded top.

Burial no. 174 at Bubastis belongs to a child, placed in a jar in a contracted position with the head to the east. The only burial good was a vessel containing five shabtis; four were in the normal mummy shape, one in everyday dress. The last may be some kind of overseer for the whole group. The clay shabtis are uninscribed and rather crude.[16] Burial no. 195 was placed in a pottery coffin. The body is on its back with its head to the north. Near the left hand was a scarab with the inscription *setep-en-amun*, 'chosen one of Amun'. At the foot of the coffin were two vessels; one of them contained eleven shabtis.[17]

An identical impression of burial customs after the Eighteenth Dynasty is gained from several burials recently excavated at Saqqara. One coffin, so decayed that it was not even possible to determine its shape, contained two skeletons: one young person and a child. Most of the burial goods found with them were jewellery – earrings, rings and amulets. One of the rings bears the name of king Sety I, so the tomb cannot be earlier than his reign, though it might be much later. There was only one bronze vessel and fragments of one pottery jar.[18] Other graves at this cemetery did not have any burial goods at all, but their relatively elaborate coffins show that their owners were not poor people. There are, for example, burials in a set of two anthropoid and decorated coffins without any additional objects. These graves are hard to date, but taking all the evidence together, they must be later than the Eighteenth Dynasty and therefore most likely belong to the Ramesside period.[19] Better dated are some graves found at Abusir and Saqqara, in which coffins survived, whose types are known from other places. Several burials were placed here in oval pits or shallow holes. The coffins in them belong to the type which shows the owner in everyday dress. While most of these are from Thebes, many simpler versions were excavated in the Saqqara/Memphis region. The lids of these latter coffins are often quite flat, while the hand, legs and garment are carved into the wood. Only the head is specially attached to the lid. The box is always undecorated; finds in these coffins are not very common. They belong to the Ramesside Period, although it is not really clear when the use of this type stops and there are signs that this kind of decoration continued until the Twenty-Second Dynasty.[20]

The evidence from the burials of the poorer classes is not a surprise. In the Ramesside period nearly all objects put in tombs were specially produced for burial. The tombs of noblemen must have been relatively richly equipped. Poorer persons were forced by lack of resources to concentrate on a few essential items (jewellery and amulets, already used in daily life?), the coffin and a few cheap shabtis and amulets. The very poor were buried without any grave goods. This is a major difference from other periods. In the Middle Kingdom most elite tombs also contained only objects produced for burial, but at that time poorer people, who could not afford such items, placed everyday objects in their tombs instead. This did not happen in the Ramesside period. New religious beliefs seem to have affected all social levels, and many parts of the country.

Although generally objects of daily use, particularly pottery, become rare in burials of the late New Kingdom, there are still some burials which contain them. At Amarna an undisturbed burial was found, in which the body was placed in a nicely painted yellow coffin. At the head end were five pots, the only burial goods. The elaborate coffin shows that the deceased must once have belonged to a higher social class.[21] At Tell el-Yahudiyeh Francis Llewellyn Griffith excavated several burials in features he called 'tumuli', but which may have been natural rather than man-made mounds. Many pottery coffins and some scarabs with kings' names of the late New Kingdom were found. Numerous pottery vessels were placed next to the burials, although it is not easy to establish an accurate picture from the published excavation report.[22] Both the Amarna and Tell el Yahudiyeh finds serve as warnings. There are doubtless local developments in burial customs around the country. At many places the use of pottery and everyday objects in burials ceases; at other places at least pottery was still placed in tombs.

Very little is known about the burials of the Twentieth Dynasty, though some can be dated to that time. Our picture of tombs and burial customs is heavily influenced by good preservation conditions at particular sites in Upper Egypt, but these may not be typical. In Lower Egypt, in the Delta, different tomb types were developed. At Bubastis a family tomb belonging to the 'viceroy of Kush' Hori was excavated (Fig. 111). The tomb is sunk into the ground with three vaulted chambers leading off each side of a central corridor. Four of these six chambers contained massive, roughly worked sarcophagi. The tomb had been looted. The few remaining burial goods included pottery and many shabtis. Nothing is known about the superstructure of this tomb, but there must once have been some kind of chapel for worshipping the dead, since chapels seem always to have been an important part of elite burials.[23] Two similar tombs were found at Esna, but they were so badly looted so that it is hard get a clear picture of them. They were built of mud-brick, though one had a stone-covered chamber in which parts of a statue of the Hathor-cow were found. The other Esna tomb is rather better preserved. The superstructure is almost like a square mastaba, with a single room in the middle. On the north side of this room there is a staircase leading down to five underground chambers. The biggest contained two roughly carved uninscribed sarcophagi. The name of the tomb owners therefore remains unknown.[24]

More conventional tombs of high officials

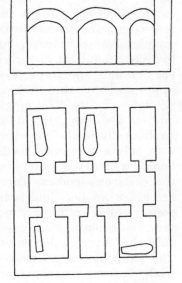

Fig. 111. Family tomb excavated at Bubastis.

of the Twentieth Dynasty are attested elsewhere. At Aniba the 'deputy of Wawat' (Lower Nubia) Pennut had a rock-cut tomb decorated with sunken relief. The tomb is datable to the reign of Ramses VI.[25] The tomb of the high priest of Nekhbet at Elkab dates to Ramses III-Ramses IX;[26] at Saqqara some free standing chapels, very similar to those of the Nineteenth Dynasty, were excavated;[27] similar chapels were found next to the mortuary temple of Ramses III at Medinet Habu.[28] At Heliopolis a lintel of the 'high steward' and 'overseer of the double granary' Khaemwaset was found, dating to the reign of Ramses III, which may have come from the funerary chapel of that official.[29] There are only a few rock-cut tombs at Thebes datable to the Twentieth Dynasty, and it is still not clear where most of the high officials of the Twentieth Dynasty were buried.

A good example of a multiple burial complex for the less wealthy at the end of the Twentieth and early Twenty-First Dynasty was excavated at Saqqara, offering a perfect view of the burial customs of rather poor inhabitants of a large city at the end of the New Kingdom. These burials were placed in the tomb of Iurudef, a middle-ranking official under Ramses II who has already been mentioned above. The tomb consists of a shaft with seven chambers over two levels, filled with seventy-two burials; twenty-seven are in anthropoid coffins, ten in rough rectangular coffins, eight simply in palm-rib mats, and finally there are about nineteen burials without any protection. The whole burial complex was plundered, but the robbers did not disturb it very much, perhaps disappointed by the lack of precious objects. The single bodies are placed almost haphazardly in the chambers with only a few grave goods. Some jewellery was found with the children's bodies. There are a few amulets and some pottery. Most coffins are not very well made, in many cases only the cover is decorated. The paintings on them are, with few exceptions, awkwardly executed. There are only a few inscriptions on

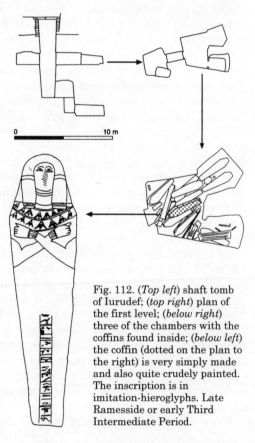

Fig. 112. (*Top left*) shaft tomb of Iurudef; (*top right*) plan of the first level; (*below right*) three of the chambers with the coffins found inside; (*below left*) the coffin (dotted on the plan to the right) is very simply made and also quite crudely painted. The inscription is in imitation-hieroglyphs. Late Ramesside or early Third Intermediate Period.

the coffins, mostly written in imitation hieroglyphs (illegible inscriptions executed by people who could not write; Fig. 112). The whole impression is that this is the burial ground of the ordinary people of Memphis. These people put all their efforts into buying a coffin. The protection of the body was clearly more important than burial goods and usually included some kind of cheap mummification and, for the richer individuals, a wooden coffin.[30]

It is not possible to identify the social level to which the individuals in this multiple burial belonged. However, some of them were laid to rest in decorated coffins and cannot therefore be the very poorest. Multiple burials of very low status people were found at Abusir, just north of Saqqara. A tomb with ten bodies was excavated in the pyramid temple of Niuserre (Fifth Dynasty). No coffins or any other protection of the bodies were found. There are only a few finds, such as some jewellery made of shells, a glass bead and a few amulets. Another mass burial was found not far away in which no objects at all were discovered. Only one of the bodies was placed on a palm mat 2.15 m long.[31] This is similar to the mats discovered in the tomb of Iurudef, so this mass grave may be more or less contemporary, although this is far from certain.

8. The Third Intermediate Period: The Peak of Coffin Production

After the death of Ramses XI, last king of the Twentieth Dynasty and of the New Kingdom, a new line of (most probably Libyan) kings began to reign in Tanis: the Twenty-First Dynasty. A related military family took power at Thebes, with its head assuming the title 'high priest of Amun' to legitimate their rule; they governed almost independently in the south, although the Tanis kings of the Twenty-First Dynasty were regarded in official inscriptions as the true kings. After over a century of this arrangement, a new family of Libyan descent took direct control of all of Egypt as the Twenty-Second Dynasty, but in the middle of that dynasty the political unity of the country disintegrated. In terms of burial customs, the period can be divided into two phases. The Twenty-First Dynasty seems to be very similar to the late New Kingdom. In the Twenty-Second Dynasty new developments can be seen.

The first half of the Third Intermediate Period

Elite burial customs at the end of the New Kingdom are still obscure, since not many tombs are preserved, whereas burials from almost all social levels are recorded from the Twenty-First Dynasty, including some undisturbed tombs of kings. In 1891 a tomb at Thebes, now known as Bab el-Gusus, was discovered. This burial place is often referred to as the 'second cache' (the 'first cache' being where many of the reburials of New Kingdom kings were found). It is a corridor about 90 m long, leading to a second slightly shorter one. At the end of the first corridor were two chambers. Both corridors and both chambers were full of coffins and other funerary material; 153 burials were found. The tomb had been opened repeatedly over a long period to insert additional coffins and related goods. Most of the burials consist of more than one coffin; altogether, 660 single coffin parts (e.g. lids, boxes, mummy boards) were found. Beside these coffins were other burial goods. There are 110 shabti boxes filled with shabtis, seventy-seven Osiris figures which mostly contained a papyrus, one Isis figure and one Nephthys figure. Thirty-two baskets were found containing provisions, and there was one bed and six boxes. More than a hundred funerary papyri were found, many placed in the Osiris figures, others found in the wrappings of the mummies. A typical burial contained two papyri, one a 'Book of the Dead' and one a text known as 'Amduat'.[1] Not all the mummies have yet been unwrapped, so the exact number of papyri placed in this tomb is not yet known. There are surprisingly few canopic jars (only sixteen), some vessels and eight wooden stelae. An average set of equipment in this mass burial therefore consists of a set of two coffins, a mummy board, a shabti box containing shabtis, a papyrus placed in the wrappings of the mummy and an Osiris figure with a papyrus in it. The people buried here belonged to a high social level, though not to the highest. Most of them are members of the Amun temple, with administrative and religious titles, precisely datable, because the mummies often had leather braces bearing the name of the king under whom the person was buried. The Osiris figures are typical of Theban burials of this period. Only a couple of examples survive from the Ramesside period, in which a wooden Osiris figure was hollowed out and used to contain a papyrus. This became standard practice in the Twenty-First Dynasty, while in the mid-Twenty-Second Dynasty funerary papyri and Osiris figures disappeared from elite tombs (see Fig. 113). The Osiris figures should not be confused with the similar statues showing the composite funerary god Ptah-Sokar-Osiris. The latter, which were not used as papyrus containers, are found in elite burials from the eighth century BC to Ptolemaic times.[2]

Fig. 113. The Osiris figure of Tanetamun.

A coffin set of the Twenty-First Dynasty usually consists of a pair of coffins with a mummy board; in poorer burials a single coffin is common. They belong to the 'yellow coffin' type (Fig. 114), in which several scenes in small vignettes were painted in bright colours on a yellow ground. This type was developed in the Eighteenth Dynasty, but at that time the vignettes were quite large and often only single figures or simple groups of figures were shown. In the Twenty-First Dynasty the painted scenes become smaller and more complex. It has been suggested that these vignettes and scenes replace paintings in tomb chapels, for there are almost no decorated chapels datable to the Twenty-First Dynasty. The coffins of the Twenty-First Dynasty are certainly among the most beautiful ever produced in Egypt. The same holds true for the funerary manuscripts placed next to many of these coffins. The 'Book of the Dead' and the 'Amduat' are the standard compositions, but there are also series of illustrations of religious motifs, such as the scene of Nut over Geb (these series are often called 'mythological papyri'). Shabtis, with increasing numbers in each set, are also very common, but their quality is often rather low, even for people of high status. They are generally made in blue faience, with inscription giving the title and name of the deceased; the shabti spell appears on only a small proportion of them.

As stated above, the people buried in the 'second cache' do not belong to

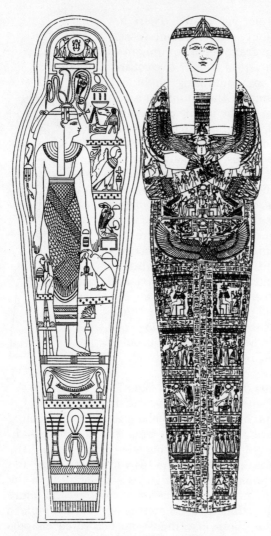

the highest social level. The ruling family is buried in another cache – known as the first or royal cache – which also contained many burials. At the end of the Twentieth Dynasty the Egyptian state became relatively poor through the loss of foreign territories and civil war, and the highest officials started to authorise the opening of the New Kingdom royal tombs. The Valley of the Kings thus began to be mined for its treasures systematically and under state control.[3] The amazing wealth found in the tombs was used by the state, some of it going to the new royal burials in Tanis, while the royal mummies were reburied elsewhere, sometimes several times. Eventually most found their final resting place (at least for 3,000 years) in a tomb at Deir el-Bahari.[4] Not only kings were buried here, but also many high priests of Amun and some members of their families. The burial equipment is similar to that in the 'second cache': two coffins, a mummy board, shabtis and shabti boxes, funerary papyri and stelae. The superb quality coffins, often gilded, demonstrate the high status of the dead. Other funerary goods such as metal vases are exceptional. Two wooden boards belonging to a certain Neskhons, wife of the high priest of Amun Pinodjem II, are also of special interest. They contain a decree by the god Amun stating that the shabtis were paid for and will only work for the owner of these boards.

Fig. 114. Coffin of the Twenty-First Dynasty.

Not everyone was buried in such mass burials. Tomb no. 60 at Deir el-Bahari is a rather small rock-cut chamber, 3 x 4 m. Originally three female members of the family of the high priest Menkheperre were laid to rest here: Henettawy, daughter of the high priest Pinodjem I and sister of Menkheperre; Djedmutesankh, who may have been the wife or daughter of the latter; and finally a second Henettawy, daughter or granddaughter of Menkheperre. The whole burial was found robbed, although some objects were still in place. The mummy of the latter Henettawy had been stuffed with sawdust to fill it out and glass inlays had been placed in the eyeholes. Seven canopic packages were found inside the body, four with a wax figure of one of the children of Horus. This was the usual way organs were treated in the Third Intermediate Period – i.e. being returned to the body after mummification; as a result, canopic jars became less common, though they are still attested for people of very high status. A pectoral had once been placed over the chest and several amulets (djed-pillars, wedjat-eyes, a scarab) were found in the neck area. Between the thighs was a papyrus scroll with the text of the 'Amduat' and inside a crude Osiris figure a 'Book of the Dead' was found.[5]

Many bodies in mass burials ascribed to the end of the New Kingdom may in fact belong to the Third Intermediate Period. The burial customs of poorer people did not change very much. Others are buried in simple decorated coffins placed as isolated graves in the desert sand. These burials are often very hard to date. The wooden coffins are normally much decayed and of low quality. The only funerary goods are amulets (which are common in child burials, but do not appear very often with adults) and there is no pottery (see Fig. 115). Burials of this type seem to be common up to Roman times.

The burial customs at Tanis, where the kings of the Twenty-First Dynasty were interred, are slightly different. The funerary complexes of

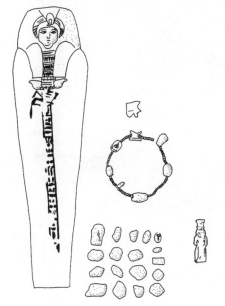
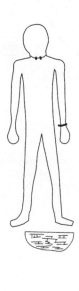

Fig. 115. Burial of a twelve- to thirteen-year-old boy in a coffin, found at Saqqara. His body was wrapped in a linen shroud and protected by a bundle of reeds. On the feet was a basket containing pieces of amber or resin, of unknown function. At the neck and around the wrist were amulets. The burial is datable by the coffin type to the end of the Twenty-First or beginning of the Twenty-Second Dynasty.

the kings, their families and some high officials have been excavated inside the Amun temple complex there. Only the underground chambers of these tombs were found; nothing of the overground chapels survived. Through the protection of the temple complex, many of these tombs were found undisturbed.[6] There are single small chambers, one for each person buried, with contemporary coffins and re-used Old, Middle or New Kingdom sarcophagi. Each person had a set of at least one sarcophagus and several coffins, although because of the dampness of the ground in Tanis only metal parts of the coffins survived. The mummy itself was covered either with a mummy board or with a mask, and richly adorned with jewellery and amulets. Other funerary goods, placed outside the coffin, included shabtis and canopic jars and chests. Many gold vessels were found in the burials. No other objects survive. As with the royal cache at Thebes, high officials were buried in the same tomb complex next to the king.

The burial of the 'high steward of Khonsu' and 'overseer of troops' Wendjebaendjed (a man of about fifty years of age) may be given as an example. It was found inside the burial complex of king Psusennes in a separate chamber. Wendjebaendjed must have been a close friend or relative of Psusennes, since several objects in his burial have a dedication inscription naming the king and in the sarcophagus of the king himself a short sword bearing Wendjebaendjed's name was found. His small burial chamber was decorated with several scenes from the 'Book of the Dead'. It was virtually filled by a huge red granite sarcophagus, which was inscribed with the titles and name of an official of the Nineteenth Dynasty. On the north side of the chamber four human-headed canopic jars were

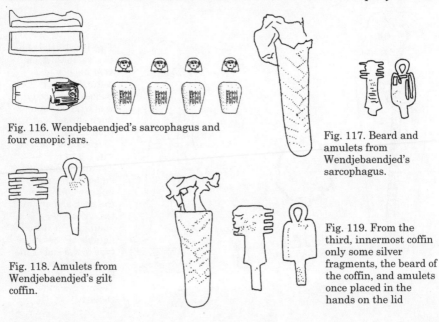

Fig. 116. Wendjebaendjed's sarcophagus and four canopic jars.

Fig. 117. Beard and amulets from Wendjebaendjed's sarcophagus.

Fig. 118. Amulets from Wendjebaendjed's gilt coffin.

Fig. 119. From the third, innermost coffin only some silver fragments, the beard of the coffin, and amulets once placed in the hands on the lid

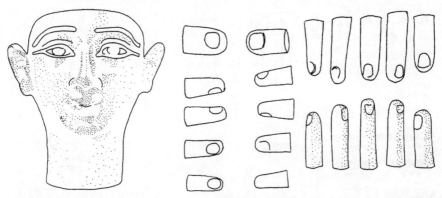

Fig. 120. The gold face of the mummy mask found over Wendjebaendjed's head.

Fig. 121. Golden covers for fingers and toes of Wendjebaendjed's mummy.

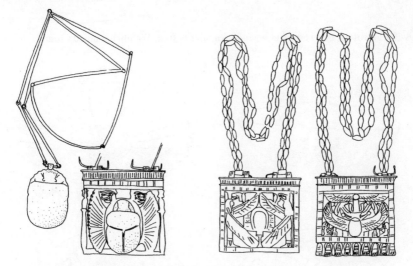

Fig. 122. Wendjebaendjed's heart scarab and three pectorals.

Fig. 123. Several small golden statuettes of gods and goddesses were found in Wendjebaendjed's tomb.

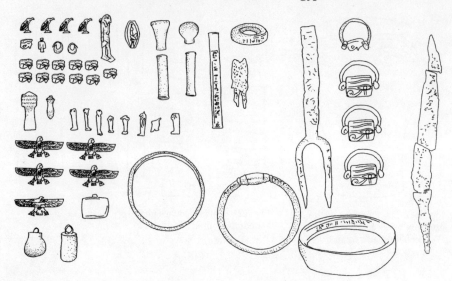

Fig. 124. Amulets, bracelets and weapon fragments from Wendjebaendjed's tomb.

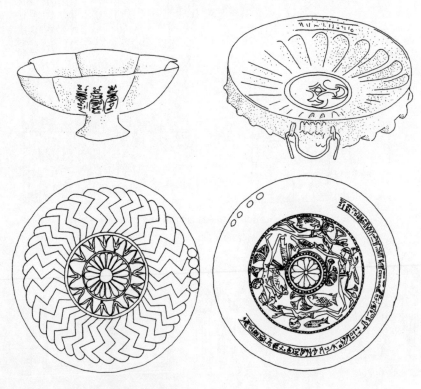

Fig. 125. Few objects in Wendjebaendjed's tomb could be called objects of daily use, but these four golden bowls belong to this category.

found; they may have been re-used, though their inscriptions refer to the 'general'.

The sarcophagus had been plastered, gilded, and then reinscribed for Wendjebaendjed; the face was adorned with a beard, and two amulets for the hands were attached. Inside the sarcophagus was a gilded coffin, of which there survived only fragments of the thin gilding and the amulets the mummy held in its hands. Inside the gilded coffin a coffin made of silver was found, not in very good condition, with only the beard and the amulets intact. The few preserved fragments show that the coffin was decorated with vignettes and inscriptions. Its decoration must have been quite similar to that of the 'yellow coffins' from Thebes. The mummy itself was covered with beads, so far the earliest attested bead net cover, later to become very popular. Fingers and toes were adorned with gold covers. On the head was placed a mummy mask, of which only the golden face has survived.

The whole mummy was covered with an array of jewellery. Special mention should be made of a set of small gold figures, including a Sakhmet, an Isis figure, and a Ptah figure in a shrine. Inside the inner coffin were also found some weapons and a set of four silver and gold vessels, which were presented by the king to Wendjebaendjed.[7] These objects – including maybe some of the jewellery – are the only items in the tomb which seem not to have been produced specifically for the burial, although a ritual function cannot be excluded for the metal vessels and weapons. All the other objects were specially made or reworked for the burial of the 'general'. As a result of the bad preservation conditions at Tanis no organic material has survived. We do not know if there was a 'Book of the Dead' placed next to the mummy, which was normal in the contemporary Theban tombs. Other objects, such as shabti boxes, would also have been utterly destroyed by the ground water.

The second half of the Third Intermediate Period

The second half of the Third Intermediate Period saw a drastic change in burial customs. In the Twenty-Second Dynasty many items typical of the Ramesside Period and the Twenty-First Dynasty disappeared (shabtis, the 'Book of the Dead'). At the same time a new type of mummy cover was introduced. Mummy masks and mummy boards were replaced by mummy cases made in cartonnage, which covered the whole body. Cartonnage was a cheap material produced from layers of gummed linen and plaster; in Ptolemaic times scrap paper – old papyrus – was used. The linen version appears first for mummy masks and other smaller funerary objects in the First Intermediate Period, but in the Twenty-Second Dynasty examples the whole body was enveloped from head to foot. They were brightly painted and used throughout the country; traces have been found at Tanis and complete examples at many other places.[8] They were always used in connection with a coffin or within a set of coffins.

The yellow coffins disappeared and were replaced by other coffin types, while the outer coffin was now often rather simple, with almost no decoration and only one line of inscription. Funerary papyri, so popular in elite burials of the Twenty-First Dynasty, started to fall out of use. The few 'Book of the Dead' scrolls datable to the Twenty-Second Dynasty belong to its first century. Other funerary objects also fell out of use or at least became less common, notably shabtis and shabti boxes. The few examples datable to this time are rather crude. Canopic jars were no longer in general use by the Twenty-First Dynasty, and they were now sometimes replaced by a set of dummy jars: models of canopic jars that are not even hollow. Tomb chapels are very rarely attested for the Twenty-First Dynasty, but there is plenty of evidence for them in the second part of the Third Intermediate Period. At Thebes many mud-brick chapels were erected on the west bank. These chapels filled the space between already existing funerary temples of kings and were also built into them. The best preserved examples were found in the Ramesseum, the mortuary temple of Ramses II in Thebes. Similar chapels have been excavated at Abydos.[9]

Although multiple burials are common for all social strata, there are still many tombs for single persons. In the area near temple of Ptah in Memphis several Twenty-Second Dynasty graves of the ruling elite of this town were excavated.[10] The tombs were built as underground limestone chambers. It is not known if any of them had an overground chapel. At least one of the burial chambers was decorated in sunken relief with scenes and chapters from the 'Book of the Dead'. This is the tomb of Sheshonq, the high priest of Ptah and son of king Osorkon II, and it was found intact. The body of Sheshonq was placed under a huge stela of the Eighteenth Dynasty, which must have been used as some kind of coffin lid. Nothing has survived of its coffin box, which may have been made of wood and therefore totally destroyed by damp. From the short excavation report it is hard to obtain a clear picture of the arrangement of the objects in the single tomb chamber. The publication gives a list of finds, but does not describe their position within the tomb. There are four canopic jars and about two hundred shabtis, many displaying high quality workmanship (Fig. 128). In the Twenty-Second Dynasty canopic jars and shabtis are no longer common burial goods, and found mainly only in the tombs of persons of the highest rank. A small stela showing Horus and Bes is of special interest, being the earliest known example of a type called the 'Horus stela'. These later became very popular as everyday amulets, but they are not typical grave goods. The mummy was richly adorned with gold. Fingers and toes had specially made gold covers, as did the sidelock – a typical attribute of the high priest of Ptah – and the penis (Fig. 126). There are many

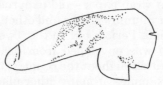

Fig. 126. Gold penis cover and side-lock cover from Sheshonq's mummy.

amulets of Osiris, Isis, Nephthys and Taweret; sixteen gold wedjat-eyes and sixteen wedjat-eyes made of lapis lazuli and agate. Two Hathor heads, one in gold, one in lapis lazuli, and a heart scarab were found on the remains of mummy (Fig. 127).[11] No pottery is published from the tomb. The burial is first and foremost remarkable for the quantity of amulets found in it. A large number of amulets had previously been a mark of kingship. Here they appear on the same scale in the tomb of a person other than the king.

Fig. 127. Hathor face made of lapis lazuli and gold, found on Sheshonq's mummy. Its function is unknown.

Tombs had been re-used since earliest times. Already in the Old Kingdom there were many mastabas re-used by later burials which changed part of the decoration and placed the name of the new body there. Especially in densely occupied cemeteries, it must often have happened been the case

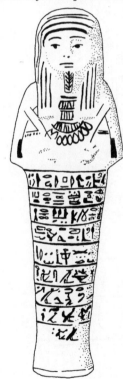

that older tombs were found by accident when a new shaft was dug. At Thebes there is clear evidence that many Middle Kingdom tombs were occupied again in the early Eighteenth Dynasty. From the Third Intermediate Period to the Ptolemaic period there seems to have been a general tendency to use older shafts or to carve new shafts in already existing burial complexes; most of the New Kingdom burial chambers in the rock-cut tombs at Thebes were now used for secondary burials. The individuals buried there sometimes have high positions and are known from monuments at other places, indicating that this was not only a practice of lower status people.[12] Although decorated tomb chapels are well attested for this period, there are not many cases where the older tomb decoration was changed. The re-use of shafts was obviously enough for these high-status people. The funerary rites and the cult of the dead may have been performed at a different place.

In the Twenty-Second Dynasty people started to bury their dead in the storerooms of the Ramesseum, as part of a huge Third Intermediate Period cemetery that sprang up at Thebes. Some of the burials were accompanied by small decorated chapels, paved with painted

Fig. 128. One of the shabtis from Sheshonq's tomb.

limestone slabs showing scenes of the tomb owner adoring gods. Burials were placed in shafts all over the area. One intact example is that of the 'god's father' and 'door opener at Karnak' Nakhtefmut. A shaft led to two disturbed burial chambers, one of which was connected to a deeper shaft. At the bottom of this, two coffins were found, both oriented with the head to the north. On the west side of the east coffin four figures of the children of Horus were found. On the north side stood an uninscribed wooden stela (compare Fig. 129). The east coffin was quite rough and contained a second coffin and then the mummy.

The west coffin belonged to Nakhtefmut; two wooden boxes containing shabtis were found next to it. The outer coffin had a jackal on the lid, while inside was a second coffin with a wooden hawk placed on it. Finally there was a third coffin covered with flowers in which the mummy, placed in a cartonnage case, was found. The cartonnage with its gilded face is brightly painted with different scenes showing gods and symbols (Fig. 130). Between the mummy and the cartonnage was a leather brace bearing the name of king Osorkon I, providing an exact date for the burial (Fig. 131). Next to the mummy there was a 'Book of the Dead' and around the neck a necklace consisting of various amulets. On the chest lay a scarab with

Fig. 129. Painted wooden stela of Pafdiu. Similar stelae have been found in many burials of the Third Intermediate Period in Thebes.

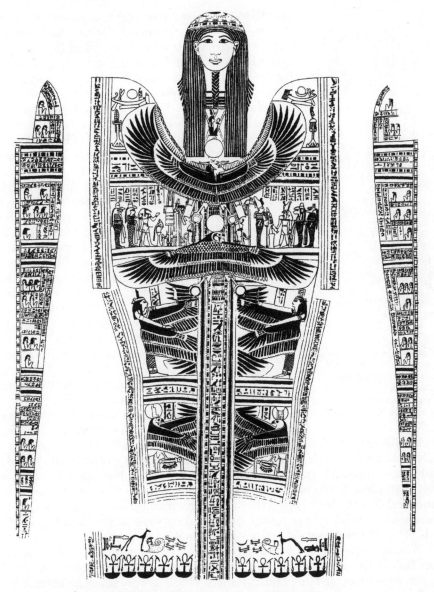

Fig. 130. Cartonnage of Nakhtefmut, Twenty-Second Dynasty.

silver wings and below it the uninscribed heart scarab. The title 'god's father' and 'door opener at Karnak' point to Nakhtefmut's having held a middle position in the administration of the Amun temple at Thebes. His burial is quite rich, if one considers the gilded face of the cartonnage and the high quality of its workmanship; it did not contain any canopic jars, but there is still a funerary papyrus. The burial therefore belongs to a

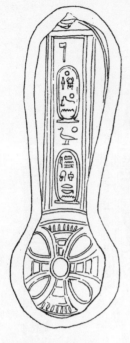

Fig. 131. Leather brace found on Nakhtefmut's mummy, bearing the name of king Osorkon I, in whose reign Nakhtefmut was buried.

transitional phase: the tomb equipment is a mixture of new (cartonnage) with older items (leather braces, funerary papyrus, shabtis).[13]

Another intact tomb also dating to the reign of king Osorkon I was excavated in 1901 in the Valley of the Kings at Thebes and provides a second example of an elite burial, although the buried persons seem to be less wealthy than Nakhtefmut. At the bottom of a small shaft a sealed chamber was found containing three coffins covered with a mass of flowers. Two of the coffins were painted black, with inscriptions executed in yellow. A third coffin was rough, to use the excavator's description, but contained a beautiful cartonnage case showing the dead in everyday dress. Coffins showing the dead in everyday dress are well known from the late Eighteenth Dynasty, and still sporadically attested in the Twenty-First Dynasty. This cartonnage case is a good example of how the decoration of a coffin might be applied to new material. All three mummies were carefully wrapped in linen, but only the last one had leather braces with the name of king Osorkon I placed on the mummy itself. There are no other burial goods: no shabtis, no canopic jars and no amulets. The titles of the dead give an idea of their social status. In one coffin was the 'singer' Iufaa, the second contained the 'chantress of Amun' Karmama, and the woman with the beautiful cartonnage was the 'mistress of the house' Tjenetqeru-sherit.[14] These titles may well indicate some middle-ranking status in the temple administration. All three may have been relatives, but any relationship between them is not stated. The high quality of the cartonnage points to the wealth of the lady buried there. The absence of other burial goods, such as shabtis, could simply reflect the burial customs of the day, but might also be explained as a sign of poverty or lack of resources.

A burial which dates a little later and may belong to people of a similar or slightly lower status was excavated in Deir el-Bahari, Thebes. An open court gave access to two tomb chambers. One was very small and contained only a set of two coffins for a certain Padiamun. The other chamber was relatively large and contained eight coffins, of which the most elaborate belonged to a woman called Irtu, daughter of Amenhotepeniuf and of the 'lady of the house' Nanun. She was placed in a single coffin which was painted with different scenes on the outside and a large Nut figure on the inside. The mummy was wrapped in linen and at the head there was a garland of leaves, adorned with flowers. Inside the wrappings were found five wax figures: the four children of Horus and a benu-bird (Fig. 132).

All the other coffins in this burial were relatively simple. They were painted black with yellow inscriptions and yellow painted decoration. The mummies were wrapped rather carelessly in linen. The only object, apart from the many flowers laid on the coffins, was a scarab found next to the elbow of one mummy. There are no other burial goods, no shabtis, canopic jars or 'Books of the Dead'.[15] The social status of these people is not known. Irtu's coffin is quite well made and inscribed, indicating that she belonged to the literate elite, and as we have seen her mother was

Fig. 132. Wax figures found on Irtu's mummy.

described as 'lady of the house'. The other persons seem to be of lower rank, and it is only possible to guess who was buried here. Considering their status, it seems more likely that these are members of her household (servants) rather than of her family.

Cemeteries excavated around Matmar and Qau-Mostagedda contained many burials most likely of farmers or at least of not very wealthy people from the countryside or a provincial town (see Figs 133-135). Luckily most of them were found undisturbed. The exact date of a single burial is often hard to determine, since few datable objects were placed in them. Most graves are single burials in shallow shafts without further chambers. The dead are laid on their back, head to the west, in anthropoid coffins with only a few grave goods: pottery and calcite vessels are rarely attested, more common are bead necklaces or strings of cowries, finger-rings, scarabs and amulets which were often found in child burials. It is therefore no surprise that Bes-figures are particularly common (Bes was the god who offered protection in childbirth). There are some graves without coffins and

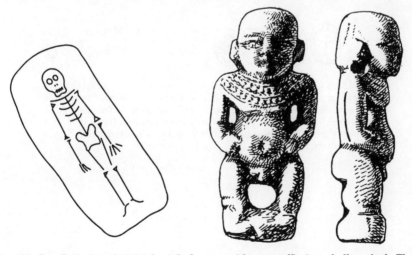

Fig. 133. Qau-Badari tomb 1531: burial of a man without a coffin in a shallow shaft. The only burial good is a dwarf figure; the exact findspot of the figure within the tomb is not recorded.

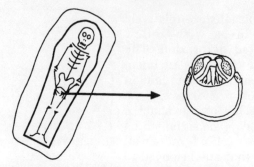

Fig. 134. Matmar tomb 1225: burial of a man in an anthropoid coffin placed in a shallow shaft. The only other grave good is a scarab mounted on a bronze ring.

without jewellery. Bad preservation often makes it impossible to determine whether the bodies were mummified, although the presence of linen is well attested in many tombs. Some people may have been buried in their everyday costume plus a few personal adornments. The coffins are the only specifically funerary objects, but again it is not possible to assess the quality of their workmanship from the surviving record. There are no shabtis or canopic jars in these graves. In general the burial customs here are similar to those of the late New Kingdom. Multiple burials are not common, in contrast to Thebes and Saqqara.[16]

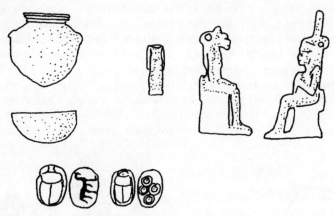

Fig. 135. Objects from Matmar tomb 726 (not to scale): burial of a woman in an anthropoid coffin – one of the better equipped burials. The scarabs were found at the hands, the vessels (only fragments) under the head. Cowries (not pictured) were the other items of jewellery found; they appear frequently in burials of the Third Intermediate Period.

9. The Late Period and Persian Domination

The fragmented political history of the last century of the Twenty-Second Dynasty is still a mystery, but in the Twenty-Fifth Dynasty Egypt was conquered by the kings of Napata (in modern Sudan). The exact nature of their rule over Egypt is still under discussion, but it brings an increase in building activity and wealth, interrupted by the Assyrian invasions of Egypt. Psamtek I, originally governor for the Assyrians, gradually achieved independence as first ruler of the Twenty-Sixth Dynasty. With this dynasty a strong line of kings again ruled over the whole of Egypt, and this is generally considered the start of the Late Period. The new stability had a very positive effect on the prosperity of the country. There is almost no other period with such a quantity of high quality large-scale royal and private monuments, though the bulk of them were Lower Egypt, where most have disappeared. In many parts of the country vast private tombs were built, but most of the finest sculptures and reliefs come from the north. The capital of the Twenty-Sixth Dynasty was Sais in the Delta, but the city and its cemeteries had been entirely quarried away by medieval times. Other major cities include Memphis and Heliopolis, and important tombs are known from both. Thebes lost its influential position, although there are also some impressive monuments of this period there. The Twenty-Fifth and Twenty-Sixth Dynasties were a time of revival. Especially in the arts, older periods often inspired the producers of new monuments.

The late Third Intermediate Period

Before discussing burials and tombs of the Twenty-Sixth Dynasty, some graves of the Twenty-Fifth Dynasty will be described. They all belong to a transitional phase between customs of the Third Intermediate and Late Period. In Thebes, at Abd el Gurna, a group of chapels was excavated, part of a huge Third Intermediate and Late Period cemetery stretching from Deir el-Bahari down to Medinet Habu. These are temple-like mud-brick structures with a pylon (a gateway with two tower-like structures) and three sanctuaries at the back. Burial shafts were found leading from the chapels, and an undisturbed tomb was found in one of these. Of the chapel itself not much has survived, but the few remains show that it once must have had three sanctuaries at the back (Fig. 136). The burials of two men, Meh-amun-peref and his son Peteramun, both titled 'servant of Amun', were found in the shaft, which leads from the middle of these sanctuaries at the back of the chapel down to a small burial chamber. The outer coffin

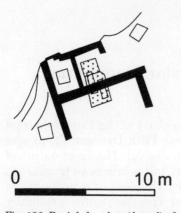

0   10 m

Fig. 136. Burial chamber (dotted) of Meh-amun-peref inside the chapel. The mud-brick built chapel is only partly preserved.

of Meh-amun-peref was box-shaped with a vaulted lid and four corner posts (compare Fig. 140). Inside were found two anthropoid coffins, both sadly very much decayed when excavated. His son Peteramun was placed in only one anthropoid coffin, which was wrapped in a mat. His mummy was decorated with a bead net. On the chest was a big faience scarab with wings, under which were visible the four children of Horus, made in beads. Between the legs of the deceased was placed a part of the body, maybe the liver. At the head of the coffin was a box with the picture of a ship on the lid. Inside the box was another mummified part of a human body. Apart from one box and the coffins nothing was found in the burial chamber, not even a shabti. The box with the organ cannot be called a canopic box; one gets the impression that for some reason there was no space left in the mummy to replace the organ and that it was therefore placed in a box which happened to be available.[1]

At Tarkhan several shaft tombs were found, probably dating from the end of the Third Intermediate Period to the Twenty-Sixth Dynasty. Most often these consisted of two or more chambers at the bottom of small shafts. These chambers, in general quite small, yielded a large number of painted wooden anthropoid coffins, each enclosed in a box coffin with vaulted lid and corner posts. Most of the coffins did not have inscriptions, and the only other finds are Ptah-Sokar-Osiris figures which are in most cases rather crudely sculpted.

Pottery was not very common in these tombs and the few examples seem to contain embalming material. One tomb of this category was found well preserved (Fig. 137). It contained, in three chambers, several box coffins with anthropoid coffins inside. Some of the coffins are inscribed, giving the name of the owners. The people buried in this tomb belong to a local elite, although no titles are recorded. The few funerary goods include some pottery and several Ptah-Sokar-Osiris figures (Fig. 138). There are also some

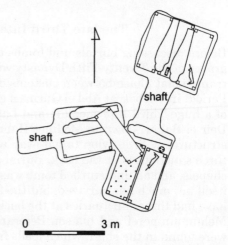

shaft

shaft

0   3 m

Fig. 137. A shaft tomb found at Tarkhan.

deep shaft tombs at Tarkan. The chambers of these were filled with mummies but without coffins. Uninscribed shabtis were found in only two of these tombs.[2]

In the Third Intermediate Period there is evidence that people again began to place some everyday objects in their tombs. Weapons and golden vessels found in the Twenty-First Dynasty tomb of Wendjebaendjed have already been mentioned in Chapter 8, but the most important recorded example is the burial of

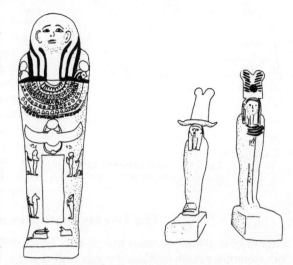

Fig. 138. The coffin of Merneith, found in a box coffin (dotted on the plan in Fig. 137), and two Ptah-Sokar-Osiris figures found in the same tomb. The original findspots of these figures inside the chambers are not recorded in the publication.

the lady Tadja in the cemetery of Abusir el-Meleq, most likely dating to the Twenty-Fifth Dynasty. The burial was placed in a small chamber at the end of a shaft about three metres deep. Within lay the body of a young girl in an outer rectangular and an inner anthropoid coffin. Around the coffin were found numerous objects: a faience box, a faience vessel imitating a basket, twenty-nine faience rings, a vessel in the shape of a duck, two head-rests and a set of musical instruments. Finally there were two statues, one of a naked woman and one of a man. Inside the coffin was a second small statue of a naked woman. Some of these finds raise special questions. One might speculate that Tadja was a particular lover of music because of the set of musical instruments. However, other burials show that it was not uncommon to place musical instruments in a tomb. Of the three small statues in the burial, two are of a nude woman. One of them might represent Tadja at an age she never reached, embodying the wish that she might become an adult woman in her next life. A similar explanation might be given for the statuette of a man placed in the tomb, who might represent her husband in the next world.[3] Finally the third statue may represent the child that she might bear in the afterlife. More or less contemporary tombs excavated at Lahun present similar burial customs. There are few undisturbed tombs from the cemetery, but the surviving burial goods include many amulets and, more importantly, there are pottery and calcite vessels. In one tomb two iron spear-heads were found (Fig. 139). The calcite vessels may be part of women's cosmetic equipment, while the spear-heads belong to burials of men. Maybe they are some kind of status symbols or personal items, worn in daily life by

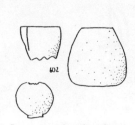

Fig. 139. Iron spear-head and calcite vessels from two tombs at Lahun, Third Intermediate Period.

these people and placed into their burials to keep their identity as man or woman, or placed there by family members. These finds appear occasionally, they are not very common. The tombs excavated at Lahun belong most likely to people of average status. The few coffins found are simple, and there are no shabtis or canopic jars.[4]

The Twenty-Sixth Dynasty

Funerary customs of the elite in the Twenty-Sixth Dynasty sometimes followed older models. Canopic jars and shabtis, rare in the second part of the Third Intermediate Period, became popular again. A set of around four hundred shabtis (one shabti for each day of the year and one to control each group of ten) is standard for elite burials. The 'Book of the Dead' was also reintroduced; only a few examples of papyri are known from this period, but the formulae are common on coffins.[5] A painted wooden figure of the composite funerary god Ptah-Sokar-Osiris, quite frequently found in the Third Intermediate Period, is now common. The normal container for the mummy of a high official is a heavy anthropoid sarcophagus, often inscribed with pyramid texts, 'Book of the Dead' chapters and other funerary texts.[6] The early examples are quite similar to sarcophagi of the New Kingdom.[7] The later ones became very broad, with a disproportionately big head. The largest sarcophagi are those found in the Saqqara shaft tombs, where they occupy almost the whole tomb chamber. They have a rectangular outline, with an interior anthropoid hollow to receive an inner sarcophagus. Inside the inner sarcophagus was a wooden coffin containing the mummy. The mummy was covered with a bead net incorporating many amulets, and the face had a gilt mummy mask. Mummy masks are often found only in these court elite tombs. By the end of the Twenty-Fifth Dynasty cartonnage fell out of use, and was replaced by a wooden inner coffin. Elite coffins of the Twenty-Fifth and Twenty-Sixth Dynasties are decorated all over with religious texts and scenes.

Burials of people of slightly lower status (but still belonging to the elite) are of course simpler. In the Twenty-Fifth and Twenty-Sixth Dynasties box coffins were used as outer container. They have a distinctive appearance with a high vaulted lid and four corner posts (Fig. 140), and are probably representations of the burial-place of the underworld god Osiris. Not surprisingly, therefore, figures of the mourning Isis (sister and wife of Osiris) and of Nephthys (sister of Osiris) were often arranged

Fig. 140. Box and anthropoid coffin of Pestjenef, approximately Twenty-Fifth Dynasty, probably from Thebes. The vaulted box coffin is an elaborate example of a type very common from about 750 BC.

around them. Similar wooden figures are occasionally known from burials dating from the Ramesside period[8] up to the Ptolemaic period. Before that time images of these goddesses were often painted on the coffins. The inner coffins – if not replaced by a cartonnage mummy case – were elaborately decorated with figures of gods and sometimes relatively long religious texts (Fig. 140). A typical feature of Twenty-Fifth and Twenty-Sixth Dynasty coffin inscriptions is an extended genealogy of the deceased. The family relations of the elite of this time are therefore well-known. A wooden anthropoid (inner) coffin is common. The mummy within was covered with a bead net and several amulets. Shabtis appear in the same high number as in elite burials, but they are often very crudely molded in faience and uninscribed. A Ptah-Sokar-Osiris figure is common.

Very few tombs of middle-ranking officials were found undisturbed, and fewer still have been published. Burials of high officials are most often single burials. Less well-to-do people were often placed together in small burial chambers, although single graves in the sand or in shaft tombs are also common. There are not many grave goods found with these burials, normally just a rough coffin and few amulets. In some cases a huge pottery vessel which contained embalming material was placed next to the burial. In general the burials of the poor in the Twenty-Fifth and Twenty-Sixth Dynasties were not very different to those of the Third Intermediate Period or the Thirtieth Dynasty. Therefore they will not be described in detail.

The kings of the Twenty-Sixth Dynasty were buried in Sais. Little is known about their tombs, but the Greek historian Herodotus saw them

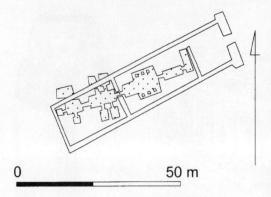

0   50 m

Fig. 141. The 'burial palace' of Padihorresnet at
Thebes. Similar and even larger funerary
complexes were built at Thebes in the Twenty-Fifth
and Twenty-Sixth Dynasties.

when he visited Egypt in the fifth century BC. They must have been similar to the royal tombs at Tanis, since Herodotus describes them as lying in the temple enclosure of Neit, the main deity of Sais.

The tombs of high officials of the Twenty-Sixth Dynasty are of various types. In Saqqara huge shaft tombs, to be described later, are common in this period. Shaft tombs of this date have also been excavated at Heliopolis, where the usual type consists of a rather small shaft leading to a decorated tomb chamber. Other tombs at Heliopolis have massively wide but not very deep shafts and contain big sarcophagi.[9] Rock-cut tombs have been discovered at Saqqara, an outstanding example being that of the vizier Bakenrenef. A similar tomb is known from Gizeh.[10] In Saqqara there is also a temple-tomb attested, of a type very similar to the New Kingdom structures at the same place.[11] Finally, there are some huge rock-cut tombs at Thebes, of a type and scale not known from earlier periods, with numerous decorated chambers cut into the ground (Fig. 141). Most of these tombs have been looted, but a number of shaft tombs from Saqqara and Abusir were found intact, giving a good impression of the burial customs of the highest officials at these places.

The main feature of the shaft tomb type in Saqqara are the huge burial shafts, up to 30 m deep and measuring as much as 8 x 10 m. At the bottom is a limestone built burial chamber. Within this was placed a huge set of sarcophagi: a rectangular outer and anthropoid inner sarcophagus. The burial chamber, its floor often completely occupied by the sarcophagi, was in many cases decorated with religious compositions such as 'pyramid texts'.

The types of objects found in such tombs are still quite limited. They are all connected with the protection of the dead:[12]

1. Four canopic jars often placed in niches on either side of the sarcophagus.
2. Shabtis made of faience or other materials.
3. Staves and sceptres.
4. Jewellery and amulets, such as wedjat-eye, ankh-sign and djed-pillar.
5. In some tombs a set of tools for the 'opening of the mouth' ceremony were found.

6. Wooden images of Osiris, Ptah-Sokar-Osiris and other deities.
7. Four 'magical bricks', which were placed in small niches at the four
   sides of the burial chamber.

The tomb of the 'overseer of the treasury of the residence, overseer of the
royal ships' Hikaemsaf was found at Saqqara, close to the pyramid of Unas
(Fig. 142). His huge tomb is a typical example of the burial of a high court
official in the Twenty-Sixth Dynasty. At the bottom of a large shaft the
vaulted burial chamber was cut. The shaft was filled after the burial with
loose desert sand. Any potential tomb robber would therefore be forced to
empty it in order to reach the burial chamber. Next to this huge shaft was
a second smaller one, evidently used for bringing the burial goods and the
mummy into the tomb. The walls of the burial chamber were covered with
funerary inscriptions, mainly pyramid texts. These may not have been
directly copied from a single Old Kingdom pyramid burial chamber, but
the idea was evidently taken from there. The chamber was almost filled
by the massive limestone sarcophagus. At the west end of it were the
canopic jars. Inside the outer sarcophagus an inner granite one was found,
and inside that a badly decayed wooden coffin. Hikaemsaf's mummy was
protected by numerous amulets, many in gold. Over the face was a gilt
mummy mask, there was a bead necklace, while the whole body was
covered with a bead net.[13]

The tomb of Tjanehebu is similar to that of Hikaemsaf (Fig. 142). The
burial chamber at the bottom of the deep shaft housed the massive
limestone sarcophagus; both chamber and sarcophagus were inscribed
with religious texts. The mummy in the sarcophagus was adorned with a
gilt mask and covered with a bead net (Fig. 143) incorporating gold
figures of the four children of Horus, images of Isis, Nephthys, Nut, and
inscribed gold plates. Around
the neck was a broad collar
incorporating a number of
amulets. Most of these gold
amulets are rather conventional, including ba-birds,
djed-pillars and wedjat-eyes.
Others are so far without
known parallel: a palm-tree,
two baboons adoring an
atef-crown, and two baboons
adoring a djed-pillar with an
atef-crown (Fig. 146). Most of
the remaining finds in the
burial chamber are typical of
the period. There are many
shabtis, the four magical
bricks and the four canopic

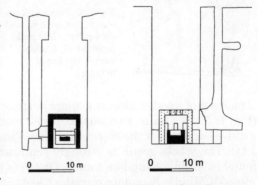

Fig. 142. (*Right*) tomb of Hikaemsaf. At the
bottom of a huge shaft is the burial chamber
(dotted) with the sarcophagus (black) inside. After
the burial the shaft was filled with loose sand.
(*Left*) shaft tomb of Tjanehebu, similar in layout
and size to that of Hikaemsaf. The burial chamber
was found intact.

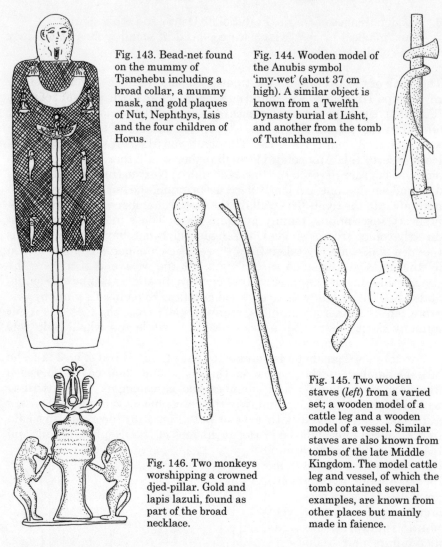

Fig. 143. Bead-net found on the mummy of Tjanehebu including a broad collar, a mummy mask, and gold plaques of Nut, Nephthys, Isis and the four children of Horus.

Fig. 144. Wooden model of the Anubis symbol 'imy-wet' (about 37 cm high). A similar object is known from a Twelfth Dynasty burial at Lisht, and another from the tomb of Tutankhamun.

Fig. 145. Two wooden staves (*left*) from a varied set; a wooden model of a cattle leg and a wooden model of a vessel. Similar staves are also known from tombs of the late Middle Kingdom. The model cattle leg and vessel, of which the tomb contained several examples, are known from other places but mainly made in faience.

Fig. 146. Two monkeys worshipping a crowned djed-pillar. Gold and lapis lazuli, found as part of the broad necklace.

jars. A set of wooden objects is more surprising, and consists of some staves (Fig. 145), two flails, two was-sceptres, model boats, a bow with arrows in a quiver and two of the objects known as 'imy-wet', symbols of Anubis (Fig. 144). The whole group is strongly reminiscent of similar wooden objects found in Middle Kingdom tombs. One gets the impression that Tjanehebu copied a Middle Kingdom burial, at least in part.[14]

Each of the tombs discussed was built for one person, although many, especially the Theban 'burial palaces', were used in later times for large groups of bodies. There are many tombs known from Saqqara and other places, which are simpler than the huge tombs of the court officials, but contain broadly similar objects to those already described. At Saqqara, shaft tombs with one to five small burial chambers are known. Most of these were found disturbed, and the remains (broken wooden coffins, shabtis, wooden figures, amulets) are in many cases disappointing. As a result not many of these tombs are well recorded or published. At Saqqara some simple mud-brick structures were found in connection with such tombs. They may belong to some kind of superstructure such as a chapel.[15] One of the disturbed tombs, consisting of several chambers, is that of the 'general' Ankh-wahibre-zaneit, which still contained a wooden coffin, 384 shabtis, four canopic jars, a rectangular box with a falcon on it and pottery, including one vessel with an inscription. In another chamber of the same tomb 367 shabtis of another person were found. From this and other evidence it seems that each chamber was used for a different person,[16] though the looting of the tomb makes it rather difficult to reconstruct the original arrangement of the tomb contents.

A bigger Late Period multiple burial was found in 1991 south of the Unas pyramid at Saqqara. The tomb was entered from a shaft about five metres deep and consists of a 10 x 3 m chamber with several side-chambers in which single burials were placed. In the floor of two of the side-chambers an anthropoid-shaped hole was carved and used as a container for a mummy. The tomb had been looted but still contained shabtis, vases with Bes-faces (very typical of the Twenty-Sixth Dynasty) and numerous small faience figures. Several hundred beads from a bead net were found on one mummy. Altogether, the remains of thirty-six individuals were recorded. The burial chamber was evidently reopened several times. Two torches found may be not burial goods, but rather tools of funerary workers.[17]

Burials with few or no funerary goods are very hard to date, and in many cases we do not have any idea of the social level to which they belong. At Saqqara and Abusir many late burials were found simply buried in the sand. The bodies were often placed in simple anthropoid coffins. Others were placed in sets of coffins. There are few inscriptions preserved on these coffins to reveal the social position of the people buried here. Nevertheless there are some quite rich burials with gold objects, which might belong to people of reasonably high social status. Pot burials are well attested for children (Fig. 147).

The period of the first Persian domination remains something of a mystery for archaeology in Egypt. There are very few monuments and even fewer tombs that can be securely dated to this time. At Saqqara a stela executed in a mixed Persian-Egyptian style has been excavated, showing the dead person on a bed with Anubis, Isis and Nephthys in one scene, and in the other dressed in Persian style. The stela was found in connection with a burial in a mummy-shaped pit carved into the desert rock, and had been re-used as cover

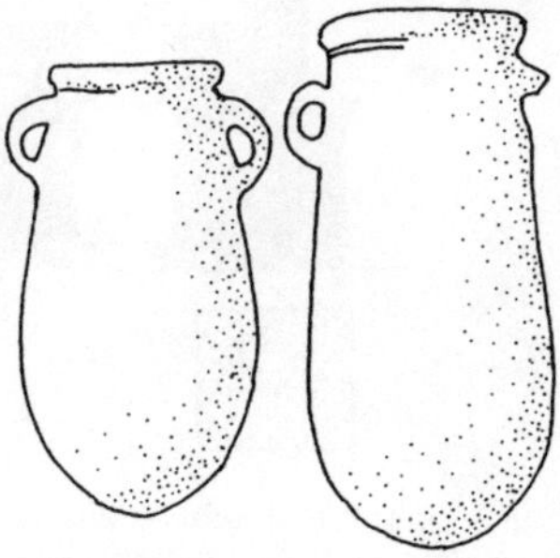

Fig. 147. Two vessels used for burials of children (*right*: 69 cm high).

for this pit tomb.[18] Its original provenance is not known. From Saqqara South there is a group of pottery coffins dated to Persian times. These coffins are mostly in rough anthropoid shape with an undecorated box and a cover on which a crude human face is modelled. Most of the coffins are uninscribed but some have an Aramaic inscription carved on the lid, usually giving just the name of the dead. There are only very few grave goods. Some of the dead had some kind of garland of plants. A pottery jar was found with only two coffins.[19] From the Aramaic (the main language of the Persian empire) inscriptions one may conclude that the people buried here were Persians living in Egypt.

The Twenty-Eighth to Thirtieth Dynasties

With the Twenty-Eighth to Thirtieth Dynasties Egypt again became independent. This is the last period in which indigenous Egyptian kings ruled the whole country. The rulers of these Dynasties were buried in the Delta cities of their families. Their tombs have been destroyed, but a few huge box-shaped royal sarcophagi have survived, some being moved to other sites in later ages. Not many tombs of court officials of the Thirtieth Dynasty are known. At Saqqara, the shaft and tomb chapel of the 'overseer of the magicians of Selket' Wennefer was excavated; he was an important person in the Thirtieth Dynasty and member of an influential family (Fig. 148). His tomb chapel consisted of a temple-like building decorated with reliefs and biographical inscriptions, very similar in its layout to the temple tombs of the New Kingdom. The shaft leading to the tomb chamber was placed in front of the chapel and contained an impressive sarcophagus in hard stone, inscribed with extended religious texts.[20]

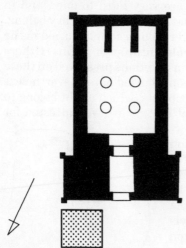

Fig. 148. Tomb chapel of Wennefer with shaft in front, Thirtieth Dynasty, Saqqara; redrawing and part-reconstruction of a sketch published without scale.

Also at Saqqara an already looted gallery was excavated with several burials of large stone sarcophagi belonging to Padineit, vizier of king Nectanebo I, and his family. The funerary complex was built into the tomb of the vizier Bakenrenef, who lived in the Twenty-Sixth Dynasty. It is not known if Padineit was related to Bakenrenef, or if he chose this place because he held the same title as the earlier high official. All the sarcophagi, which were mostly of fine limestone, were placed in niches in the gallery. Only that of Padineit was made in black basalt. They were all box-shaped with a slightly trapezoidal outline and a vaulted lid, inscribed in some examples, while the interiors were mummiform. Other remains include many shabtis, amulets and a bead net, which must have been placed on a mummy. Inscribed mummy bandages are of special interest.[21] The custom of inscribing mummy shrouds with chapters of the 'Book of the Dead' is first attested at the end of the Seventeenth/beginning of the Eighteenth Dynasty; later New Kingdom examples are rare. In the Thirtieth Dynasty and in the Ptolemaic period, the linen on the mummy was again inscribed with chapters from the 'Book of the Dead', but this time on the narrow bandages wrapped directly around the body. Most of the known inscribed bandages are not from controlled excavations and are therefore hard to date. The examples in the tomb of Padineit constitute one of the few cases in which they were found in context and are therefore datable; others belong on prosopographical grounds to the Ptolemaic period.

Sarcophagi are not securely attested for the Persian period, but they appear again in the Thirtieth Dynasty. At the moment it is very hard to date them more precisely. It is often impossible to assign a single sarcophagus (or coffin) securely to the Twenty-Sixth Dynasty, the Thirtieth Dynasty or early Ptolemaic times. In general it can be said that the examples of the Thirtieth Dynasty and early Ptolemaic period are made in hard stone. The head becomes bigger than ever, giving the features a slightly distorted appearance (Fig. 149). In the Thirtieth Dynasty huge box-shaped sarcophagi appear, covered with vignettes of underworld books such as the Amduat or the 'Book of the Dead'. Some follow the model of royal sarcophagi of the New Kingdom, giving the impression that these older prototypes were directly copied.

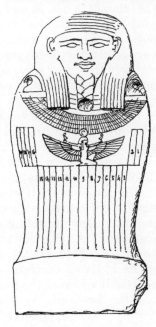

One important undisturbed burial of the Thirtieth Dynasty or early Ptolemaic period was found in Thebes in the Twenty-Sixth Dynasty burial palace of the 'high steward' Ankh-Hor. The tomb of Ankh-Hor is a vast monument belonging to one of the most influential people in Upper Egypt at the time. After the Twenty-Sixth Dynasty, maybe even shortly after the burial of Ankh-Hor, other people came here to bury their dead. Most of these later burials have been plundered and only a few remains of coffins and other objects have been found. Only one of the later intrusive burials was found intact, that of the 'priest of Amun-Re lord of the thrones of the two lands' Wahibre. It was placed in a small chamber just big enough for the coffin. This chamber was covered with a massive limestone block on which most of the burial goods were placed. The main find was a group

Fig. 149. Granite sarcophaghus found at Gizeh.

119

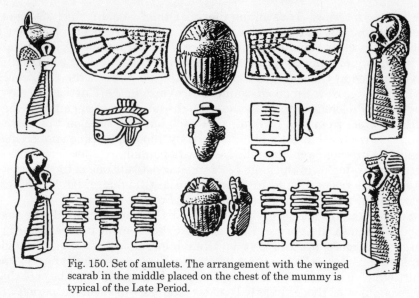

Fig. 150. Set of amulets. The arrangement with the winged scarab in the middle placed on the chest of the mummy is typical of the Late Period.

of 374 shabtis (many preserved only in fragments), which lay in no clear order on the middle of the limestone block. Next to these were some pottery vessels and copper tools, which might have been used for the mummification. There were two wooden statues, one of the mourning Isis, the other of Osiris. Remarkably there were seven animal mummies placed at the end of the chamber: two falcons, two ibises, a cat and two young dogs. Examination of their bodies revealed that some of the animals died very young; they were presumably killed for this burial, and it is therefore unlikely that they were pet animals. Other finds in the chamber include one mould-like object, which contained embalming material and a tile with a seal impression.

Under the huge limestone block on which these objects were found were Wahibre's two anthropoid coffins. Both were decorated all over with small pictures of gods, though the decoration is imperfectly preserved. The inner coffin was simpler; under a broad collar ran several lines of hieroglyphs of 'Book of the Dead' chapter 72, a very common spell on coffins at this time.

The mummy itself was adorned with a partly gilded mummy-cover made of cartonnage, under which was found a bead-net cover adorned with many amulets, including a winged scarab and the four children of Horus (compare Fig. 150). Under the mummy cover there was also a 'Book of the Dead' scroll placed in the area of the lower torso. The mummy itself lay on its back, hands on chest. In the mummy bandages gold leaf was found, especially covering the fingers and the toes, maybe also the eyes, the legs and the forehead. Wrapped in with the bandages were many amulets, mainly made of faience. These included small figures of various gods, scarabs, a few animals, which might also represent gods, parts of the body (heart, phallus, wedjat-eyes), and djed-pillars and tiyet-signs. An amulet in the form of a head-rest was found at the neck.[22]

At Abydos Petrie excavated several tombs of broadly the same period, although it is almost impossible to give an exact date. He found several vaulted chambers with many burials. Each of the excavated chambers seems to belong to one family with the burials of several relations together. Tomb G 50 was dated by Petrie to the Thirtieth Dynasty, because one person placed in the tomb was named Djedher (Teos), the name of a Thirtieth-Dynasty king, but also popular later. The burial chamber was completely filled with clean sand, maybe on purpose to protect the bodies. Four sarcophagi were found in the chamber. One contained only a mummy, without any ornaments or jewellery. A second belonged to Djedher. His mummy was placed inside the sarcophagus on a wooden tray. The mummy itself was adorned with many amulets similar to those mentioned above with Wahibre. Under the head was placed a bronze hypocephalus, i.e. a disc decorated with religious texts and images. Next to the sarcophagus two boxes filled with shabtis were found. They contained 198 and 196 figures respectively, while several quite rough shabtis were found just lying around. Another sarcophagus contained two wooden coffins, one inside the other. The mummy was decorated with partly gilded elements of cartonnage. A 'Book of the Dead' was placed on the mummy and a hypocephalus was found under the head (compare Fig. 151).

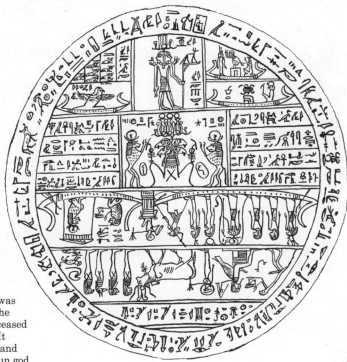

Fig. 151. This hypocephalus was placed under the head of the deceased as an amulet. It bears symbols and scenes of the sun god.

The fourth sarcophagus belonged to Nebtaihyt, wife of Djedher. It contained an outer wooden coffin and a wooden statue of Osiris. The statue contained a bundle of papyrus, maybe a substitute for a more expensive 'Book of the Dead'. An inner coffin had almost totally rotted away when Petrie found it. The mummy was again covered with different cartonnage elements and the head lay on a hypocephalus.[23]

At Saqqara burials were found placed in coffins and then laid directly in the sand, with one concentration at the pyramid complex of Teti, an area partly occupied in the Late Period by some huge temples. 123 burials were excavated here by the Egyptian Exploration Society, but similar groups were found at several other places at Saqqara. The limited datable material points to a period of about 400-300 BC for these graves. Most of them consist of a simple painted coffin with one line of inscription. The coffins are made of wood, but some parts of them are plastered in mud. They are painted, showing the dead person with a wig and a broad collar. On the body of the lid the four children of Horus sometimes appear, while the box is normally not decorated. Only very few of the bodies buried in these coffins have been mummified, maybe indicating that the people did not have great resources. The only finds are amulets strung and worn as necklaces, but even these are not common and mostly placed in the burials of children (Fig. 152).[24] The social status of the people buried here is not really known. However, the use of coffins – although very simply made – shows that these people were not the very poorest. The lowest social classes are perhaps to be found elsewhere: some burials at Abusir evidently belong to them. They show that poor people also started to re-use older funerary goods, although this is not exclusively a sign of impoverishment: in many cemeteries it is well attested that objects found in older tombs – maybe even in the course of digging a new tomb – were placed in the new burial. A poorly prepared mummy, oriented with its head to the west, was found under the lid of a typical Late Period coffin, without the box.[25] The date of the burial is uncertain, but the coffin lid can be dated exactly to the late Twenty-Sixth Dynasty, since the name of king Apries appears on it. The burial itself could date from any time from the late Twenty-Sixth Dynasty to Ptolemaic times. There are no other finds around to help fix a date.

Fig. 152. Burial of a child, *c.* 400-350 BC, Saqqara. The body in the coffin was adorned with amulets.

10. Ptolemaic Egypt:
The Hellenistic World and Egyptian Beliefs

After the conquest of Egypt by Alexander the Great, unprecedented numbers of Greeks came to Egypt and settled there. The new capital, Alexandria, must have been a purely Greek city in early Ptolemaic times, though it was to become more and more Egyptian. It is no great surprise that Greeks in Egypt buried their dead according to their own traditions. In Alexandria many entirely Greek-style funerary stelae have been uncovered, inscribed in Greek and decorated in relief or painting with a scene showing the dead person. The

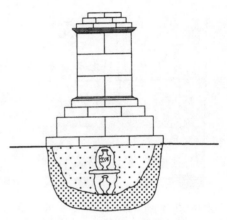

Fig. 153. Urn burials under a small mausoleum in the necroplis of Shatbi Alexandria.

main difference must have been in the treatment of the body – embalmed in the Egyptian tradition, but cremated in the Greek. Numerous funerary urns have been found in excavations in the city, demonstrating the popularity of this distinctly un-Egyptian burial style at least for the Ptolemaic period (Fig. 153). In other places in Egypt the Greeks buried their dead in wooden coffins decorated in fully classical style, showing that not all these immigrants chose cremation.

The Egyptians went on burying their people in fully Egyptian style, to the extent that it is often impossible to determine whether a burial belongs to the Thirtieth Dynasty or the early Ptolemaic period. These Egyptian burials of the early Ptolemaic Period show no Greek influence. There are still shabtis, Ptah-Sokar-Osiris figures, canopic boxes, amulets, hypocephali, and funerary papyri (Fig. 154). Elements covering the body, including mummy masks, now became very popular, and there are still many coffins in Egyptian style. But by the end of the Ptolemaic period most of these objects had disappeared. There are no more shabtis, canopic jars or Ptah-Sokar-Osiris figures, demonstrating a dramatic change in burial customs. There are still problems in charting the development in detail. Very few burials and tombs of this period have been carefully excavated and published. Almost no elite burials have been found intact and

 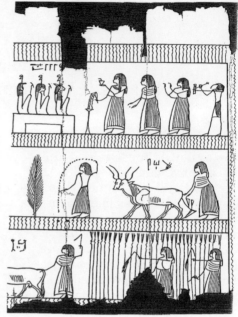

Fig. 154. Two examples from the 'Book of the Dead' of Neshorpre, Ptolemaic Period. (*Left*) Vignette to chapter 16, with the adoration of the sun. (*Right*) part of the vignette to chapter 110, showing the dead ploughing in the fields of the Underworld.

recorded.[1] Only a few examples can therefore be given here to illustrate what is known about this period.

Mummy masks, mummy coverings and coffins are the most remarkable objects of funerary production in Ptolemaic times. The mummy masks, now more common than before, are in general still purely Egyptian. For the coffins the same holds true, though one has the impression that finely decorated coffins became less important, while attention was very much focused on the mummy mask and other elements placed directly on the wrapped body. There are many well produced early Ptolemaic sarcophagi, mainly anthropoid and made of limestone, similar to examples of the Thirtieth Dynasty. By contrast, there are almost no decorated sarcophagi in late Ptolemaic times, and coffins at this time became generally rather crude. Coffins and (decorated) sarcophagi were often placed inside a rough limestone outer sarcophagus. In many cases the mummy was just put directly into such a roughly worked stone box. The mummy itself was adorned with a mummy mask and panels of cartonnage, or fully enclosed by a cartonnage cover. These elements are often very fine; the focus of artistic production was clearly on these parts of the burial. Late Ptolemaic coffins and mummy cases sometimes display unusual iconography showing the dead with many royal attributes.[2] The underlying idea is presumably that the dead person was identified with Osiris, ruler of the underworld. There are many different styles in funerary culture attested at this time. Some of these differences may reflect change over time, but there are also doubtless contemporary local traditions, with each regional centre developing its own style.

Not much is known about chapels or tomb architecture. There are still numerous stelae from burials, but it is not clear whether they were placed next to the coffins in the burial chambers or in some kind of chapel above single burials. Painted burial chambers are documented from some places such as Abydos or Atfih.[3] Their precise date is often uncertain.[4]

One closely datable burial group was found in the 1820s in Thebes and belongs to a priest of Amun named Hornedjitef, who lived under Ptolemy III (245-222 BC). It can be taken as a good example of an elite burial of the early Ptolemaic period. The burial consisted of an outer and an inner coffin, the mummy, adorned with a mummy mask and partly gilded mummy coverings enclosing the body from the shoulders to the feet, a hypocephalus placed under the head, a Ptah-Sokar-Osiris figure, a canopic box and a 'Book of the Dead' scroll. The shrine-shaped box decorated as a canopic box contained only potsherds, while the mummy still had its internal organs; the box therefore seems to be dummy canopic equipment. It is one of the latest known examples.[5] The 'Book of the Dead' remained very popular in the Ptolemaic period; several hundred can be dated to this time. Many of them come from Thebes, others from Saqqara, and a handful from other sites such as Akhmim.

Not all elite burials were placed in specially prepared burial chambers. In Abusir the intact grave of a certain Khet-Hap was found. His coffin, decorated on the lid with a long inscription, was placed directly into the ground between two Old Kingdom walls. The mummy itself was covered with elements of gilt cartonnage: on the head there was a mask, on the chest a broad cartonnage collar and under it a seated figure of Nut. Other cartonnage pieces showed the four children of Horus, Isis and Nephthys. The mummy was wrapped in thick linen, the arms crossed over the chest, the head oriented to the west.[6] As in many similar cases, it is not possible to give an exact date for this burial. The gilding of several parts of the equipment demonstrates Khet-Hap's wealth.

A cemetery used throughout Ptolemaic and Roman times has been excavated at Qau el-Kebir in Middle Egypt. Several hundred tombs were found. Most of them had already been heavily looted when excavated. However, together they give a fair impression of the burial customs of a provincial community in both periods. Some burials belong to relatively wealthy people, the ruling elite of this provincial town. The body of a certain 'overseer of the oil makers' (?) Petosiris was placed in a rough box-shaped sarcophagus, of which only the head end was rounded. An inner sarcophagus was made of limestone and bore an inscription. Inside were traces of the mummy with faience amulets over it. The whole group was placed in a chamber together with six other bodies, four in similar box-shaped sarcophagi, two placed only in anthropoid coffins. Another tomb (no. 234) contained four rough box-shaped sarcophagi; two contained an anthropoid sarcophagus, one of which bore a painted inscription. The bodies inside the sarcophagi were mummified and protected with amulets. This set of coffins, found undisturbed, was placed at the bottom of a shaft. No other burial goods were found beside the sarcophagi. Both tombs are hard to date, but an early Ptolemaic or even Thirtieth Dynasty date seems plausible. At this site many coffins, but also mummies on their own, were placed in rough stone sarcophagi. These sarcophagi, mummy-shaped on the inside, are typical of the Ptolemaic period and are found at many places in Egypt, often in great numbers in tombs, showing that multiple burials are still very common.

Most other burials at Qau el-Kebir are simpler. Pottery coffins with round ends are common. In many cases they were covered with bricks or even only with rough stones. The bodies of the deceased were often found mummified; some were found as skeletons and it is not clear whether this is just the result of bad preservation (the ground is very damp in Qau el-Kebir), or whether there was really no treatment of the body. The mummies were sometimes adorned with a cartonnage mummy mask and a separate foot case made of the same material. The only funerary goods are faience amulets placed on the mummy. Although many of the dead buried here do not belong to the poorest classes, there are no signs of shabtis or canopic chests. The only other funerary objects found were some roughly made stone offering tables. One of those excavated was placed directly on the coffin, but the others were found without context, making it impossible to say whether the one example is an exception, or whether this was the normal place for the offering table. Such tables were originally used in the cult of the dead and one would expect to find them standing on top of a burial.[7]

Well preserved cemeteries of Ptolemaic date have also been found in Lower Nubia, which was at this time a border zone between Egypt and the kings of Meroe in the Sudan. A cemetery excavated in 1908-9 contained several burials, each placed in a small chamber entered by a short sloping passage. The richer examples contained a rough stone sarcophagus with a decorated wooden coffin. The mummy within was in a cartonnage casing or covered with separate panels of this material. Some of the tombs contained more than one burial. Clay coffins are sometimes found in place of a sarcophagus; some of the clay examples are roughly painted with floral patterns. The tombs do not contain many grave goods. In one of them the mummy of a calf was placed next to the dead person.[8] The publication of these tombs is much abbreviated, so it is not possible to say whether the mummies were adorned with amulets, as found in Qau el-Kebir. Poorer tombs contained a mummy on its own, without any coffin or cartonnage. These mummies are simply wrapped in linen and placed into the small chamber. It is impossible to say how common such burials are. The short publication focuses on the richer tombs. Only one example is given of such poorer tombs, and it is not stated whether it is typical or exceptional.[9]

11. Egypt in the Roman Empire

In 30 BC Egypt was conquered by the Romans and became a part of their empire. In the Ptolemaic period, funerary culture had remained, at least for the Egyptians, almost entirely traditional. Under Roman rule, Egyptian elements became rare, and were steadily replaced by stylistic elements from the Mediterranean world or by objects in a new hybrid style. Much recent research has been devoted to funerary culture in Roman Egypt, but with a focus on individual aspects, such as the well-known painted Fayum portraits and mummy masks. There has been less attention to the broader picture of burial customs in general. As a result we are well informed on some details of elite burials, while other important features are totally unexplored. It is therefore hard to give more than a rough outline of development of the time.

At the beginning of the Roman period, mummy masks and cartonnage cases covering the whole body were in general still executed in Egyptian style, and it is in most cases not possible to distinguish them from late Ptolemaic examples.[1] The first century AD saw the introduction of masks in the tradition of classical Greek and Roman art. The first step in this direction was the appearance of one or two elements, such as curls over the forehead – a feature borrowed from classical art – while all other parts of the decoration remained purely Egyptian.[2] Also in the first century AD mummy portraits were introduced. These are wooden panels painted with a depiction of the head and shoulders of the deceased, as in Roman art, executed using the Roman encaustic technique (mixing pigments in wax), and showing a more or less naturalistic image of the dead person. The custom of placing painted portraits on a mummy is found at cemeteries in the north (Marina el-Alamein, 100 km west of Alexandria), around the Fayum, where most have been found, and at some sites in Middle Egypt, such as Antinoopolis. At none of these cemeteries were the painted portraits very common: Petrie recorded that at Hawara he found on average only one or two per hundred mummies. The custom was therefore evidently restricted to relatively few people. Even less common are linen mummy shrouds painted in Roman style with a life-size picture of the dead person. A burial at Hawara in which a mummy mask and portraits were found together suggests that the mask was more expensive, since the man was found with a gilded mummy mask (Fig. 155) whereas the children and wife were buried with painted portraits.[3] Roman-period mummy masks have been found in all parts of Egypt and seem to have been more common than the painted portraits, although their better chances of survival may be distorting the picture. There is also a group of cartonnage cases found

Fig. 155. Gilt plaster mummy mask found at Hawara. The man is depicted in classical style. Three painted portraits were found together with this mask, proving that painted portraits and mummy masks were used side by side.

at Akhmim and Abusir el-Meleq, showing the deceased in everyday Greek-Roman style dress. Other examples from Akhmim are formed in Egyptian style (like a mummy) with only a few Greek elements. These mummy cases may date to around 50 BC to 50 AD, although an exact dating is not possible at present.[4]

The development of anthropoid coffins is far less clear; at some point they ceased to be produced, but it is not known when. There are some examples showing the dead person in everyday dress, but these are exceptional.[5] The elaborate mummy masks and cartonnage cases evidently took over the function of coffins, and most mummies adorned with masks or placed inside a cartonnage case were found without a coffin. The few Roman-period coffins from Egypt are in most cases rectangular, and at least till the second century AD they still have hieroglyphic inscriptions and scenes executed in Egyptian style.[6] Many of them have a plaster head attached at the lid. This seems to be some kind of echo of the tradition of anthropoid coffins of earlier periods.[7] The marble relief sarcophagi popular elsewhere in the Roman empire seem not to have been generally adopted in even the most Hellenised cities of Egypt such as Alexandria, although a few examples have been found there.

The 'Book of the Dead' was replaced by short funerary compositions such as the 'Book of Breathing', attested from the mid- to late first century BC to the second century AD.[8] The mummified bodies in the so-called Soter group (a family burial found at Thebes, early to mid-second century AD) were each equipped with two small sheets of papyrus bearing such texts, one for the head and one for the feet. There may be some funerary papyri that are later in date, but in general the tradition of placing a text in the tomb next to the mummy stopped at this time.[9]

Amulets made of faience are still attested, but no longer common, and seem also to disappear in the first century AD, while gilded wax amulets strung on deep reed frames seem to have continued in production into the second century. Shabtis and canopic jars are not attested at all. However, everyday objects appear again in many tombs. These are often small luxury articles, for example cosmetic items such as glass vessels are common in burials of women. Sometimes women were adorned with personal jewellery, such as ear-rings and finger-rings.[10] These are typical products of the Roman world and do not look much different from jewellery found in other parts of the Roman empire. At some cemeteries the custom of providing the dead person with a coin (for the ferryman in the underworld – a Graeco-Roman custom) is widespread.[11] At other places people did not place coins next to the dead. One might surmise that the former cemeteries contained more Hellenised people. Research into Roman-period burials has concentrated on the equipment of mummified bodies, but there must also have been quite a high number of burials of poorer people who could not afford mummification and who were just buried, maybe in everyday dress, in shallow holes in the ground. Other people may have decided for cultural or religious reasons not to be mummified. One such burial was found near Tarkhan and contained the body of a woman with a gold ring and a golden necklace of high quality. Next to her some alabaster vessels were found. She was certainly not of low status, and one wonders if she was a Roman or Greek lady, who did not want to follow Egyptian burial customs.[12]

There is a wide range of burial customs in Roman Egypt[13] reflecting many local traditions. One group of graves at Denderah can be quite closely dated. They were placed, like the Ptolemaic graves discussed in Chapter 10, in small chambers reached by a staircase. Most of the tombs had been heavily looted. Nevertheless there are important remains left, such as stelae showing the deceased in front of gods of the underworld. Many mummies also had a small label, also known from many other sites, with the name and affiliation of the deceased and, in a few instances, a date, showing that some of the deceased were buried in early Roman times (early to mid-first century AD).[14] The amulets found are quite important, since they are among the latest glazed examples produced in Egyptian style.[15] Although they are only loosely connected with the dated mummy labels, it seems that all burials that can be dated to later periods do not have any glazed amulets.

The extensive cemeteries at Qau el-Kebir also yielded many tombs dating to the Roman period. Although the graves had been heavily looted, the whole site gives a fair impression of burial customs in a provincial corner of the Roman empire. The return of everyday objects to the tombs is the most distinctive feature (though the custom is attested in the Ptolemaic period, but seems then to be restricted to the Greek population). In many burials various kinds of pottery (including lamps), glass and faience vessels were found. There are several buildings at Qau el-Kebir which might be termed mausolea. At the edge of the fertile land a chain of small buildings was erected. They are quite similar, being two metres square and built of mud-brick. The walls are plastered white; many of them must have been vaulted. There is quite often a niche in one of the walls, which may have contained a lamp, though this is only a guess. Many of the buildings did not have an entrance. Others had an entrance and were decorated with paintings in entirely Roman style showing a standing figure of the owner of the chapel. Burials were placed under these chapels. In one of them many skeletons were found just under the floor. In another,

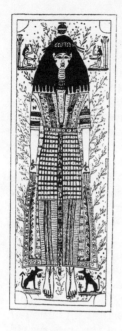

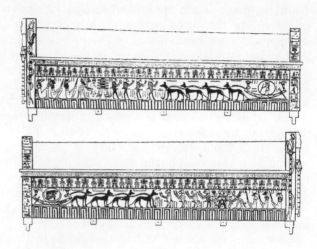

Fig. 156. The coffin of Padiimenipet from the Soter family burial, decorated entirely with Egyptian motifs. The inside of the lid (*left*) bears a painted figure of Nut.

just one burial was excavated in the middle of the room in a pottery coffin, without any further objects.

Such mausolea are relatively common in Roman Egypt. However, they differ from place to place, suggesting that there were particular local styles and developments. At er-Rubayat (ancient Philadelphia) a number of stone-built underground burial places were found. One of them was round with a circular central hall and several burial chambers arranged around it. At Hawara several chapels were excavated. The burials were placed under the floor. The buildings themselves were sometimes decorated with paintings. At Abu Billo the tombs were rectangular or square with a barrel-vaulted roof. Some of these tombs were painted, and many of them had a niche on the east side, usually containing a stela in Roman style. Similar tombs have been excavated at Saqqara.[16] At Douch (Dakhla oasis) underground burial chambers were found in which the dead person was placed on a funerary bed.[17]

The Soter group, mentioned above in connection with papyri, is an assembly of coffins found in a Ramesside Theban tomb. The dead were placed in box coffins painted with traditional Egyptian motifs and zodiacs (Fig. 156). The mummies themselves were wrapped in shrouds with a

Fig. 157. Padiimenipet's mummy.

130

frontal picture of the deceased. On the chest
was placed a cartonnage element in the shape
of a seated winged Nut and a bead net with a
winged scarab and the four children of Horus,
all made in beads (Fig. 157). Next to the
mummies were placed two sheets of papyrus
with funerary compositions. The traditional
funerary equipment is here reduced to the
coffin (and, in other examples, the mummy
masks), the bead net and two short funerary
papyri. Some everyday objects were also found,
such as necklace or comb.[18]

One last example of burials in Egyptian style
may be presented here. A cemetery developed
in the mid-second century AD at Deir el-Bahari.
Most of the burials found here were placed
directly in the sand in re-used coffins or
massive pottery vessels. Only some of them are
mummified. A few are well prepared, with a
mummy mask, though this was not a common
feature among these burials (twenty-six
mummy masks are known so far from the
cemetery – the total number of burials is not
known). The mummies were found completely
swathed in linen and adorned with many
flowers. The mummy masks show the deceased
in Roman dress with Roman jewellery and often
holding a glass vessel. At the bottom of these masks traditional Egyptian
motifs of two jackals, flowers and a Sokar bark (Fig. 158) are depicted,
while the rest of the decoration is more Roman.[19]

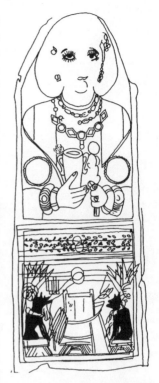

Fig. 158. Mummy cover found
at Deir el-Bahari (mid-third
century AD).

*

I end my short description of 5,000 years of burial customs in Ancient
Egypt here, at the beginning of the third century AD. Strong connections
to Pharaonic traditions did persist in some areas in later times, but in
other areas Pharaonic culture became less important, making this a
reasonable end point for our survey.

Notes

Abbreviations

The abbreviations used here are those adopted in the *Lexikon der Ägyptologie (LÄ)* (Wiesbaden), with the exception of the following:

Emery, *Great Tombs II* = W.B. Emery, *Great Tombs of the First Dynasty II*, London (1954)
Emery, *Archaic Egypt* = W.B. Emery, *Archaic Egypt*, Edinburgh (1961)
Garstang, *Burial Customs* = J. Garstang, *The Burial Customs of Ancient Egypt*, London (1907)
Hayes, *Scepter I* = W.C. Hayes, *The Scepter of Egypt* I, New York (1953)
Jéquier, *Tombeaux de particuliers* = G. Jéquier, *Tombeaux de particuliers contemporains de Pepi II*, Fouilles à Saqqarah, Cairo (1929)
Jørgensen, *Catalogue Egypt I* = M. Jørgensen, *Catalogue Egypt I (3000-1550 BC)* Ny Carlsberg Glyptotek, Copenhagen (1996)
Junker, *Gîza I* = H. Junker, *Gîza I. Die Mastabas der IV. Dynastie auf dem Westfriedhof*. Wien/Leipzig (1929)
Mummies & Magic = S. D'Auria, P. Lacovara & C.H. Roehrig (eds), *Mummies & Magic: The Funerary Arts of Ancient Egypt*, Boston (1988)
el-Sawi, *Tell Basta* = A. el-Sawi, *Excavations at Tell Basta*, Prague (1979)
Tooley, *Egyptian Models* = A. Tooley, *Egyptian Models and Scenes*, London (1995)
Willems, *Chests of Life* = H. Willems, *Chests of Life*, Mededelingen en Verhandelingen van het Vooraziatisch-Egyptisch Genootschap 'Ex Oriente Lux' XXV, Leiden (1988)

Preface

1. This attitude seems to me the typical view of a modern upper-class person (the Egyptologist) of the lower classes in antiquity, and goes along with such views as the idea that farmers in ancient Egypt were very happy to join in building the pyramids – they would have enjoyed doing a boring or arduous job, however slight the material reward.

1. Early Farmers and State Formation

1. J. Eiwanger, *LÄ* IV, 94-5.
2. F. Debono & B. Mortenson, *El Omari*, Archäologische Veröffentlichungen 82, Mainz (1990), pp. 73-7.
3. I. Rizkana & J. Seeher, *Maadi IV: The Predynastic Cemeteries of Maadi and Wadi Digla*, Archäologische Veröffentlichungen 81, Mainz (1990), pp. 69-93.
4. Rizkana & Seeher, op. cit., p. 89.
5. G. Brunton & G. Caton-Thompson, *The Badarian Civilisation*, BSAE 46, London (1928), pp. 14-15 (tomb 5705, 5735), pls VII-VIII, XXVII.
6. J. de Morgan, *L'âge de la pierre et les métaux*, Recherches sur les origines de l'Égypte I, Paris (1896).

7. G. Dreyer, *Um el-Qaab I*, Archäologische Veröffentlichungen 86, Mainz (1998).

8. R. Friedman, *JARCE* XXXVI (1999), pp. 6-7; J.H. Taylor, *Death and the Afterlife in Ancient Egypt*, London (2001), p. 47, fig. 19.

2. Early Dynastic Egypt:
The Tomb as the House of the Afterlife

1. K. Bard, *From Farmers to Pharaohs*, Sheffield (1994); T. Wilkinson, *State Formation in Egypt: Chronology and Society*, BAR International Series 651, Oxford (1996), pp. 69-85.

2. Emery, *Great Tombs II*, pp. 140-2.

3. Emery, *Archaic Egypt*, pp. 56, fig. 17, 133, fig. 78, pl. 18.

4. R. Stadelmann, *Die ägyptischen Pyramiden*, Mainz (1991) (2nd ed.), p. 20, n. 56 (with further literature).

5. Emery, *Great Tombs II*, pp. 146-7.

6. Emery, *Great Tombs II*, pp. 147-8.

7. W.M.F. Petrie, *The Royal Tombs of the First Dynasty I*, London (1900), p. 8 ('a few beads'); Petrie, *The Royal Tombs of the First Dynasty II*, London (1901), pl. XXXVIII.9-29. One of the tombs with beads (W51) belonged to a woman called Aha-Neith (Petrie, op. cit., pl. XXVI).

8. Emery, *Archaic Egypt*, p. 82, figs 43-45.

9. W.M.F. Petrie, G.A. Wainwright & A.H. Gardiner, *Tarkhan I and Memphis V*, BSAE 23, London (1913); W.M.F. Petrie, *Tarkhan II*, BSAE 25, London (1914).

10. G.A. Reisner, *The Development of the Egyptian Tomb down to the Accession of Cheops*, Cambridge (1936).

11. A. Scharff, *Grab als Wohnhaus in der ägyptischen Frühzeit*, Sitzungsberichte der Bayerischen Akademie der Wissenschaften, philosophisch-philologische und historische Klasse 1944/6, München (1947).

12. J.E. Quibell, *Excavations at Saqqara (1911-12): The Tomb of Hesy*, Cairo (1913).

3. The Old Kingdom: The Age of the Pyramids

1. N. Tacke, *MDAIK* 52 (1996), pp. 307-36.

2. Y. Harpur, *The Tombs of Nefermaat and Rahotep at Maidum*, Prestbury, Cheltenham (2001).

3. N. Alexanian, *Dahschur II, Das Grab des Prinzen Netjer-aperef. Die Mastaba II/1 in Dahschur*, Archäologische Veröffentlichungen 56, Mainz (1999).

4. Junker, *Gîza I*, pp. 23-38 (on the stelae); A.M. Roth, *JARCE* XXX (1993), pp. 33-55; A. Bolshakov, *Man and his Double in Egyptian Ideology of the Old Kingdom*, Ägypten und Altes Testament 37, Wiesbaden (1997), pp. 37-9 (on the changes in general).

5. F. Tefnin, *Art et magie au temps des pyramides: l'enigme des têtes dites 'de remplacement'*, Monumenta Aegyptiaca 5, Brussels (1991).

6. Junker, *Gîza I*, passim, especially, pp. 100-31.

7. W.M.F. Petrie, E. Mackay & G.A. Wainwright, *Meydum and Memphis (III)*, BSAE 18, London (1910), p. 26, pl. 18.

8. B. Lüscher, *Untersuchungen zu ägyptischen Kanopenkästen*, Hildesheimer Ägyptologische Beiträge 31, Hildesheim (1990), pp. 2-4; J.H. Taylor, *Death and the Afterlife in Ancient Egypt*, London (2001), pp. 66-7; C.M. Firth & B. Gunn, *Excavations at Saqqara, Teti Pyramid Cemeteries I – text*, Cairo (1926), p. 126 (the inscriptions on Kagemni's canopic jars); royal inscribed examples: Cairo CG 5020-2.

9. G.A. Reisner, *A History of the Giza Necropolis II, The Tomb of Hetep-Heres the Mother of Cheops: A Study of Egyptian Civilisation in the Old Kingdom*, Cambridge, Massachusetts (1955).

10. V. Vasilijevic, *Untersuchungen zum Gefolge des Grabherrn in den Gräbern des Alten Reiches*, Beograd (1995), pp. 105-9; E. Brovarski, in *Studies in Honor of William Kelly Simpson*, edited by P. der Manuelian, Boston (1996), pp. 117-55.

11. For a typology and discussion of these statues, see M. Hill, *Egyptian Art in the Age of Pyramids*, edited by D. Arnold, New York (1999), pp. 386-95.

12. Cairo CG 111; Tooley, *Egyptian Models*, p. 24, fig. 14.

13. Cairo CG 113.

14. Oriental Institute of the University of Chicago 10628, 10645.

15. The tomb is discussed by S. Rzepka, *MDAIK* 56 (2000), pp. 353-60 (she comes to the conclusion that not Babaf, but an unknown woman was buried here).

16. N. Alexanian in *Stationen, Beiträge zur Kulturgeschichte Ägyptens, Rainer Stadelmann gewidmet*, H. Gusch & D. Polz (eds), Mainz (1998), p. 19, no. 8.

17. G.A. Reisner, *A Provincial Cemetery of the Pyramid Age, Naga-ed-Dêr III*, Oxford (1932), pp. 212-13.

18. S. Hassan, *Excavations at Gîza, 1929-1930*, Oxford (1932), p. 44.

19. S. Hassan, *Excavations at Gîza, 1930-1931*, Cairo (1936), pp. 141-50; good colour photographs of some of the gold jewellery are published in C. Aldred, *Jewels of the Pharaohs*, London (1971), pls 4-5.

20. S. Hassan, *Excavations at Gîza III, 1931-1932*, Oxford (1941), pp. 240-1.

21. Reisner, op. cit., p. 242.

22. G. Brunton & R. Engelbach, *Gurob*, BSAE 41, London (1927), pp. 6-7, pls IV-VII.

4. The Late Old Kingdom to the Middle Kingdom: The Development of a Funerary Industry

1. The tomb of a certain Impy found at Gizeh is not yet fully published.

2. Many other mastabas of the elite were still built at Gizeh and Saqqara. In the Old Kingdom courtiers were not always buried next to the king they served; A.M. Roth, *JARCE* XXV (1988), pp. 201-14.

3. M. Verner, *ZÄS* 124 (1997), p. 77, pl. V.3.

4. *Mummies & Magic*, p. 93, no. 25 (the burial is datable by seal impressions to Djedkare Issesi).

5. *Mummies & Magic*, pp. 93-4, no. 26 (the date is not secure).

6. Jéquier, *Tombeaux de particuliers*, pp. 26, 28-9, fig. 29.

7. W. Seipel, *Ägypten: Götter, Gräber und die Kunst, 4000 Jahre Jenseitsglaube*, Linz (1989), p. 71, no. 40a&b.

8. This kind of food container is sporadically found in later periods too (Middle Kingdom tomb/cenotaph of Senusret III at Abydos, also made in calcite) but is only regularly part of the tomb equipment in the New Kingdom (and then made of wood). After the New Kingdom they seem to disappear.

9. *Mummies & Magic*, p. 81, no. 11; R. Van Walsem, *OMRO* 59 (1978-9), pp. 193-249.

10. Jéquier, *Tombeaux de particuliers*, p. 57, fig. 63.

11. L. Borchardt, *Das Grabdenkmal des Königs Ne-user-re*, Leipzig (1907), pp. 126-34 (the tomb); M. Verner, *The Mastaba of Ptahshepses, Reliefs I/1 Abusir I*, Prague (1977), p. 44, no. 45; p. 45 n. 13 (about the family of Kahotep).

12. For similar palettes see S. Tawfik, *GM* 30 (1978), pp. 77-87.

13. el-Sawi, *Tell Basta*, no. 161.

14. M. Vallogia, *Le mastaba de Medou-nefer, Balat I*, FIFAO 31, Cairo (1986).

15. Vallogia, op. cit., 74-8; On the importance of these texts: H. Willems, *Chests of Life*, p. 245.

16. G. Lapp, *Typologie der Särge und Sargkammern von der 6. bis 13. Dynastie*, SAGA 7, Heidelberg (1993), pp. 30-1.

17. G. Jéquier, *Tombeaux de particuliers*, pp. 94-104, pl. XII; A. Tooley, *Egyptian Models*, pp. 53-4; earliest crew: models of Idu (H. Junker, *Gîza VIII, Der Ostabschnitt des Westfriedhofs II*, Wien (1947), pp. 91-6), for the date: B. Schmitz (ed.), *Untersuchungen zu Idu II, Giza*, Hildesheimer Ägyptologische Beiträge 38, Hildesheim (1996), p. 42.

18. Garstang, *Burial Customs*, pp. 31-2.

19. W.M.F. Petrie & G. Brunton, *Sedment I*, BSAE 34, London (1924), pp. 2-3, pls VII-XII.

20. Jørgensen, *Catalogue Egypt I*, p. 94.

21. H. Junker, *Gîza VIII, Der Ostabschnitt des Westfriedhofs II*, Wien/Leizig (1947), p. 92, pls XVI-XVII.

22. B. Schmitz (ed.), *Untersuchungen zu Idu II*, p. 42; possibly contemporary is the burial of Ikhekhi, which also contains wooden models: E. Drioton & J.-P. Lauer, *ASAE* 55 (1958), pp. 216-17, pls X-XII.

23. Jørgensen, *Catalogue Egypt I*, pp. 96-7, no. 35; J. Bourriau, *Pharaohs and Mortals*, Cambridge (1988), no. 90; A. Tooley, *Egyptian Models*, pp. 9-10, fig. 10; p. 22, fig. 12; p. 24, fig. 15; Most of the models are now in Cairo, CG 236-54.

24. H. Willems, *Chests of Life*, p. 50.

25. G. Brunton & R. Engelbach, *Gurob*, BSAE 41, London (1927), pp. 7-8, pls X-XII. My first idea, that this pendant is Minoan, was not confirmed by further research. I am grateful to Robert Schiestel (Vienna) for bringing Egyptian parallels to my attention.

26. See S. Seidlmayer's discussion in J. Assmann, G. Burkard & W.V. Davies (eds), *Problems and Priorities in Egyptian Archaeology*, London/New York (1988), pp. 175-217; Seidlmayer, *GM* 194 (1988), pp. 25-51.

27. Ulrike Dubiel, *Studien zur Typologie, Verteilung und Tragesitte der Amulette, Perlen und Siegel im Alten und Mittleren Reich anhand der Graeberfelder der Region zwischen Qau el-Kebir und Matmar*, forthcoming.

28. R. Lepsius, *Denkmäler*, II, Bl. 148.

29. Tooley, *Egyptian Models*, passim.

30. Garstang, *Burial Customs*, p. 126, fig. 123; *Mummies & Magic*, p. 113, fig. 60.

31. Garstang, *Burial Customs*, p. 62, fig. 48.

32. Hayes, *Scepter I*, p. 266, fig. 173.

33. Garstang, *Burial Customs*, p. 87, fig. 77, p. 95, fig. 85; W.M.F. Petrie & G. Brunton, *Sedment I*, BSAE 34, London (1924), pl. XXVI; H.E. Winlock, *Models of Daily Life in Ancient Egypt*, New York (1955), pls 30-1.

34. Tooley, *Egyptian Models*, pp. 23-4, fig. 15.

35. Winlock, op. cit., pl. 32.

36. Garstang, *Burial Customs*, p. 76, fig. 64.

37. Jørgensen, *Catalogue Egypt I*, no. 54.

38. Jørgensen, *Catalogue Egypt I*, no. 54.

39. Garstang, *Burial Customs*, p. 133, fig. 131; *Mummies & Magic*, p. 113, fig. 61; Hayes, *Scepter I*, p. 265, fig. 172; Winlock, op. cit., pls 25-7.

40. *Mummies & Magic*, p. 114, fig. 62.

41. Tooley, op. cit., p. 45, fig. 43.

42. Tooley, op. cit., pp. 46-7, fig. 45.

43. Tooley, op. cit., pp. 47-8, fig. 46.

44. Garstang, *Burial Customs*, p. 158, fig. 158; p. 161, fig. 164.

45. *Mummies & Magic*, p. 116, fig. 72.

46. Winlock, op. cit., pls 9-12.

47. Winlock, op. cit., pls 13-16.

48. W.M.F. Petrie & G. Brunton, *Sedment I*, BSAE 34, London (1924), pl. XVII; A. Tooley, *Egyptian Models*, pp. 56-7, fig. 59.

49. K. Sowada, T. Callaghan & P. Bentley, *The Teti Cemetery at Saqqara. IV, Minor Burials and Other Material*, Australian Centre for Egyptology: Reports 12, Warminster (1999), 13 (94/2).

50. Sowada, Callaghan & Bentley, op. cit., 15 (94/10).

51. Hayes, *Scepter I*, pp. 303-5.

52. Garstang, *Burial Customs*, pp. 54-65, 211; pl. VII (no. 1).

53. E. Fiore-Marochetti, *JEA* 86 (2000), pp. 43-50.

54. J.-E. Gautier & G. Jéquier, *Mémoire sur les Fouilles de Licht*, Cairo (1902), p. 98, fig. 115, 101, fig. 123.

55. J.-E. Gautier & G. Jéquier, op. cit., 65, fig. 76; J. de Morgan, *Fouilles a Dahchour. Mars-Juin 1894*. Vienne (1895), p. 16, fig. 18.

56. E. Fiore-Marochetti, *GM* 144 (1995), p. 49.

57. K. Michalowski, Ch. Desroches, J. de Linage & J. Manteuffel, *Fouilles Franco-Polonaises III, Tell Edfou 1939*, Cairo (1950), pp. 70-1, 324, pl. XLVII (16).

58. D. Arnold, *Der Tempel des Königs Mentuhotep von Deir el-Bahari III: Die königlichen Beigaben*, AV 23, Mainz (1981), p. 49, pl. 62a.

59. W.C. Hayes, *Scepter I*, pp. 322-3, fig. 210; Garstang, *Burial Customs*, p. 93, fig. 83; *Mummies & Magic*, 111.

60. *Mummies & Magic*, p. 111, fig. 56 and J. Taylor, *Death and the Afterlife in Ancient Egypt*, London (2001), p. 68, fig. 34; V. Raisman & G.T. Martin, *Canopic Equipment in the Petrie Collection*, Warminster (1984), no. 3 (two similar canopic jars of the 'overseer of the sealers' Wahka; against the statement of the two publications the provenance of the jars is not known, the assignment to Qaw el-Kebir is made only on the basis of the name Wahka, which is also very common at other places of the Middle Kingdom).

61. Garstang, *Burial Customs*, pp. 92-3.

62. H.E. Winlock, *The Slain Soldiers of Neb-Hetep-rê' Mentu-hotpe*, New York (1945); Franke, *BiOr* 45 (1988), p. 102; R. Müller-Wollermann, *Discussions in Egyptology* 13 (1989), p. 110 (on the dating).

63. Willems, *Chests of Life*, pp. 64-5.

64. Garstang, *Burial Customs*, p. 237; pictures of the arrows: pp. 159-160, fig. 161-2.

65. H. Schäfer, *Priestergräber und andere Grabfunde vom Ende des Alten Reiches bis zur griechischen Zeit vom Totentempel des Ni-user-re*, Leipzig (1908), pp. 99-100, 152-64.

66. Lady William Cecil, *ASAE* 4 (1903), pp. 69-70; H. Willems, *The Coffin of Heqata*, Orientalia Lovaniensia Analecta 70, Leuven (1996), p. 362.

67. M. Raven, *OMRO* 63 (1982), pp. 7-34.

68. D. Arnold, *Antike Welt* 3 (1991), p. 156, fig. 8.

69. Willems, *Chests of Life*, pp. 161-4.

70. Hayes, *Scepter I*, 272, fig. 178; for the dating compare W. Grajetzki, *Die höchsten Beamten der ägyptischen Zentralverwaltung*, Berlin (2000), pp. 130, 248.

71. G. Daressy, *ASAE 1* (1900), pp. 26-32; Similar boats are depicted on the pyramidion of king Khendjer (Thirteenth Dynasty); G. Jéquier, *Deux pyramides du moyen empire*, Fouilles à Saqqarah, Cairo (1933), p. 21, fig. 17.

72. Garstang, *Burial Customs*, p. 225, tomb no. 500.

73. Hayes, *Scepter I*, p. 312, fig. 203 (Hapy-ankhtifi, from Meir); pp. 311-12 (Nebet-hut, from Meir); Garstang, *Burial Customs*, p. 175, fig. 181, J. Taylor, *Egyptian Coffins*, London (1989), p. 25, fig. 16; J. Bourriau, *Pharaohs and Mortals*, Cambridge (1988), no. 72, pl. III. 3 (Userhet, from Beni Hasan); L. Bareš, *ZÄS* 118 (1991), pp. 94-6 (a burial at Abusir).

74. W.M.F. Petrie, *Gizeh and Rifeh*, BSAE XIII, London (1907), 12, pls XA-E; M. Murray, *The Tomb of Two Brothers*, Manchester (1910).

75. H. Schäfer, *Priestergräber und andere Grabfunde vom Ende des Alten Reiches bis zur griechischen Zeit vom Totentempel des Ni-user-re*, Leipzig (1908), pp. 18-39.

76. R. Engelbach, *Riqqeh and Memphis VI*, BSAE 25, London (1915), pl. XL (the tomb register in the publication provides only the types and not the numbers of vessels found).

77. For well preserved small mastabas see D. Randall-Maciver & C.L. Woolley, *Buhen*, Philadelphia (1911), pl. 82.

78. W.M.F. Petrie, *Gizeh and Rifeh*, BSAE XIII, London 1907, pp. 14-20, pls XIV-XXII.

79. C. von Pilgrim, *Elephantine XVIII, Untersuchungen in der Stadt des Mittleren Reiches und der Zweiten Zwischenzeit*, Archäologische Veröffentlichungen 91, Mainz (1996), p. 174.

80. von Pilgrim, op. cit., 165; Similar burials are also known from other periods: A. Herold, *Ägypten und Levante* IX (1999), pp. 85-100 (early Ramesside).

5. The Late Middle Kingdom to the Second Intermediate Period: New Magical Rites

1. J. Bourriau in *Social Aspects of Funerary Culture in the Egyptian Old and Middle Kingdom,* edited by H. Willems, Leuven, Paris, Sterling (Virginia), OLA 103 (2001), pp. 1-20.

2. 'Court type' burials: four princesses near the pyramid of Amenemhat II: J. de Morgan, *Fouilles à Dahchour 1894-1895*, Vienna (1903), pp. 46-74; Senebtisi: A.C. Mace & H.E. Winlock, *The Tomb of Senebtisi at Lisht*, New York (1916; reprint 1973); Iunefer: W.M.F. Petrie, G.A. Wainwright & E. Mackay, *The Labyrinth, Gerzeh and Mazghuneh*, BSAE 21, London (1912), p. 36; Zawadjet: R. Engelbach, *Riqqeh and Memphis VI*, BSAE 26, London (1915), pp. 23-5, 29; Neferuptah: N. Farag & Z. Iskander, *The Discovery of Neferwptah*, Cairo (1971); Nebuheteptikhered, Hor: J. de Morgan, *Fouilles à Dahchour Mars-Juin 1894*, Vienna (1895), pp. 87-115; Sesenebef: J.E. Gautier & G. Jéquier, *Mémoire sur les Fouilles de Licht*, Cairo (1902), pp. 74-9; Zatwerut: Arnold, *Egyptian Archaeology* 9 (1996), pp. 38-9. 'Court type' burials in general: B. Williams, *Serapis* 3 (1975-6), pp. 41-55; C. Lilyquist, *Serapis* 5 (1979), pp. 28-9.

3. D. Arnold, *Der Pyramidenbezirk des Königs Amenemhet III. in Dahschur. I, Die Pyramide*, Archäologische Veröffentlichungen 53, Mainz (1987).

4. J. de Morgan, *Fouilles a Dahchour, Mars-Juin 1894*, Vienne (1895), pp. 88-106; the finds from the tomb are now in the Cairo Museum, the tomb is discussed in detail in S. Aufrère, *BIFAO* 101 (2001), pp. 1-41; For pottery found in royal tombs of the Middle Kingdom, see D. Arnold, *MDAIK* 38 (1982), pp. 57-8; S. Allen in C. Eyre (ed.), *Proceedings of the Seventh International Congress of Egyptologists*, OLA 82, Leuven (1998), pp. 39-48.

5. Hayes, *Scepter I*, p. 224, fig. 140.

6. J. Taylor in S. Walker & M.L. Bierbrier, *Ancient Faces: Mummy Portraits from Roman Egypt,* London (1997), p. 11.

7. S. Quirke in A. Loprieno (ed.), *Ancient Egyptian Literature, History and Forms*, Probleme der Ägyptologie 10, Leiden/New York/Köln (1996), p. 390.

8. Earl of Carnavon & H. Carter, *Five Years' Explorations at Thebes*, London/New York/Toronto/Melbourne (1912), pp. 54-5; the tomb is briefly discussed by J. Bourriau, in S. Quirke (ed.), *Middle Kingdom Studies*, New Malden (1991), pp. 19-20.

9. Garstang, *Burial Customs*, p. 146, fig. 144.

10. Garstang, *Burial Customs*, pp. 113-14, pl. V.

11. Anthes, *MDAIK* 12 (1943), pp. 6-15.

12. R. Engelbach, *Harageh*, BSAE 28, London (1923), pp. 2-3.

13. G. Brunton, *Qau and Badari III*, BSAE 50, London (1930) p. 10.

14. N. Reeves, *Ancient Egypt: The Great Discoveries* London (2000), p. 27. The tomb is discussed by Winlock, who doubts that the coffin and the canopic box belong together, *JEA* 10 (1924), pp. 270-1.

15. D. Polz, *Antike Welt* 2002 (3), pp. 289-95.

16. W.M.F. Petrie, *Qurneh*, BSAE XVI, London (1909), pp. 6-10, pls XXII-XXIX.

6. The New Kingdom: Death in an Affluent Society

1. C. Näser in B. Arnst, I. Hafemann & A. Lohwasser (eds), *Begegnungen: Antike Kulturen im Niltal*, Leipzig (2001), pp. 373-8; Gift-giving was a common economic principle in Ancient Egypt; J. Janssen, *JEA* 68 (1982), pp. 253-8.

2. There is at least one anthropoid coffin with the 'Book of the Dead': A. Grimm & S. Schoske, *Im Zeichen des Mondes*, Munich (1999), p. 19.

3. S. Ikram & A. Dodson, *The Mummy in Ancient Egypt*, London (1998), p. 143, fig. 160 (X-ray of a mummy with a heart scarab); M.-P. Vanlathem, *CdÉ* LXXVI (2001), pp. 48-56.

4. C. Lilyquist in *Ancient Egypt, the Aegean, and the Near East: Studies in Honour of Martha Rhoads Bell*, edited by J. Phillips, San Antonio, Texas (1997), fig. 3.

5. Lilyquist, op. cit., figs 4-5, 10-11.

6. Lilyquist, op. cit., figs 6-7. Other similar tombs: D. Polz, *MDAIK* 51 (1995), pp. 207-25; Polz in J. Assmann, E. Dziobek, H. Guksch & F. Kampp (eds), *Thebanische Beamtennekropolen*, SAGA 12, Heidelberg (1995), pp. 25-42; maybe also R. Mond, *ASAE* 6 (1905) pp. 80-1.

7. M. Barwik, *Études et Travaux* XVIII (1999) pp. 8-33 (typology and dating of the 'white coffins').

8. A. Lansing & W.C. Hayes, *BMMA* XXXII (1937), Ja. sect. II, pp. 4-39; *PM* I, 2 (2) pp. 669-70.

9. W.M.F. Petrie, *Illahun, Kahun and Gurob*, London (1891, pp. 21-4, pls XXVI-XXVII.

10. Garstang, *Burial Customs*, pp. 218, figs 114-15, 117a, 128, 155-6, 159-61.

11. R. Engelbach, *Harageh*, BSAE 28, London (1923), pl. LXIII (273 is here wrongly ascribed as 272); for further information on tomb 273 compare the tomb card (published on a CD-Rom by the Petrie Museum).

12. W.M.F. Petrie, *Six Temples at Thebes 1896*, London (1897), p. 8.

13. T. Säve-Söderbergh & L. Troy, *New Kingdom Pharaonic Sites: The Finds and the Sites*, The Scandinavian Joint Expedition 5: 2-3. Uppsala (1991), p. 256.

14. Säve-Söderbergh & Troy, op. cit., p. 271.

15. Säve-Söderbergh & Troy, op. cit., p. 264.

16. Säve-Söderbergh & Troy, op. cit., p. 259, pl. 157.

17. T.M. Davis, *The Tomb of Iouiya and Touiyou*, London (1907; reprint 2000); T.M. Davis, *The Funeral Papyrus of Iouiya*, London (1908; reprint 2000).

18. E. Schiaparelli, *Relazione sui lavori della Missione Archeologica Italiana in Egitto (anni 1903-1920). Vol. II: La tomba instatta dell'architetto Cha nella necropoli di Tebe,* Turin (1927).

19. G. Daressy, *ASAE* 2 (1901), pp. 1-13.

20. D. Aston, *OMRO* 74 (1994), pp. 21-54: a typology of shabti-boxes. Type I (p. 22) is attested earlier; but it is in fact a box-shaped model coffin.

21. G.T. Martin, *MDAIK* 42 (1986), pp. 109-29.

22. B. Bruyère, *Rapport sur les fouilles de Deir el Médineh (1933-1934)*, Cairo 1937, FIFAO 14, pl. X.1, XII; compare W. Grajetzki, *GM* 150 (1996), pp. 68-9; and J. Taylor in *Colour and Painting in Ancient Egypt,* edited by W.V. Davies, London (2001), p. 178, nn. 37, 39.

23. Compare the scenes of the *sed* festival in the tomb of Kheriuef: Epigraphic Survey, *The Tomb of Kheruef*, Theban Tomb 192, OIP no. 102, Chicago (1980), pl. 47.

24. G.T. Martin, *The Hidden Tombs of Memphis*, London (1991), pp. 178-85.

25. F. Abitz, *Statuetten in Schreinen als Grabbeigaben in den ägyptischen Königsgräbern der 18. und 19. Dynastie*, Wiesbaden (1979).

26. B. Bruyère, *Rapport sur les fouilles de Deir el Médineh (1928)*, Cairo (1929), pp. 36-73.

27. Other parts of this New Kingdom cemetery: C.M. Firth & B. Gunn, *Excavations at Saqqara: Teti Pyramid Cemeteries I – text*, Cairo (1926), pp. 66-83.

28. K. Sowada, T. Callaghan & P. Bentley, *The Teti Cemetery at Saqqara. IV, Minor Burials and Other Material*, Australian Centre for Egyptology, Reports 12, Warminster (1999), p. 13 (94/3).

7. The Late New Kingdom: Reduction to Essentials

1. The first yellow coffin may be datable to the reign of Amenhotep III; A. Dodson, in *Deir el-Medina in the Third Millennium AD*, R.J. Demarée & A. Egberts (eds), Leiden (2000), pp. 89-100.

2. For good colour photographs of some objects see E. Hornung & B.M. Bryan (eds), *The Quest for Immortality: Treasurers of Ancient Egypt*, Munich/London/New York (2002), pp. 143-53, nos 61-8.

3. M.A. Corzo (ed.), *Nefertari, Luce d'Egitto*, Rome (1994), pp. 191-7, nos 49-57; H.C. Schmidt & J. Willeitner, *Nefertari*, Mainz (1994), pp. 94-9.

4. E. Feucht, *Das Grab des Nefersecheru*, Theben II, Mainz (1985), pp. 125-48

5. T.G. James in J. Assmann, *Das Grab des Amenemope (TT 41)*, Theben III, Mainz (1991), pp. 267-73.

6. D. Polz in Assmann, op. cit., pp. 244-67.

7. G.T. Martin, *The Hidden Tombs of Memphis*, London (1991), p. 111, fig. 73.

8. J.-L. Chappaz, *CdE* 61(1981), pp. 32-40.

9. M. Chaban, *ASAE* II (1901), pp. 137-40; G. Brunton, *Mostagedda and the Tasian Culture*, London (1937), p. 136 (190), pl. LXXIX. There is the tomb of an offcial serving Tutankhamun at Akhmim: B.G. Ockinga, *A Tomb of the Reign of Tutankhamun at Akhmim*, ACER 10, Warminster (1997).

10. A. Kamal, *ASAE* 16 (1916), pp. 73-4, 79.

11. B.G. Ockinga & Y. al-Masri, *Two Ramesside Tombs at El Mashayikh II*, Warminster (1990), p. 36.

12. J. Osing, *Das Grab des Nefersecheru in Zawyet Sultan*, Archäologische Veröffentlichungen 88, Mainz (1992).

13. el-Sawi, *Tell Basta*, no. 57.

14. el-Sawi, *Tell Basta*, nos 16, 23, 30, 80, 144, 153, 175, 182, 139, 149.

15. *Mummies & Magic*, 160-61, nos. 112-13; Farid, *ASAE* 61 (1973) pp. 22-4.

16. el-Sawi, *Tell Basta*, pp. 84-5, fig. 206-7; a summary on shabtis in lower-class burials is given by F. Poole in *Egyptological Studies for Claudio Barocas*, edited by R. Pirelli, Naples (1999), pp. 95-113.

17. el-Sawi, *Tell Basta*, pp. 90-1, figs 221-4, 219.

18. K. Sowada, T. Callaghan & P. Bentley, *The Teti Cemetery at Saqqara. IV: Minor Burials and Other Material*, Australian Centre for Egyptology, Reports 12, Warminster (1999), pp. 24-5 (95/41).

19. Sowada, Callaghan & Bentley, op. cit., pp. 34 (95/77), 37 (95/90).

20. My own observation on the Munro excavations at Saqqara in 1995/6; Unas causeway: J. Leclant & G. Clerc, *Orientalia* 66 (1997), p. 263; for a good picture of such a coffin, see M. Verner, *Abusir III: The Pyramid Complex of Khentkaus*, Prague (1995), pl. 3, figs 13-14.

21. J.H. Taylor & A. Boyce in B.J. Kemp, *Amarna Reports III*, Occasional Publications 4, edited by A.J. Spencer, London (1986), pp. 118-46.

22. F.L. Griffith, *Mound of the Jews and the City of Onias*, London (1890), pp. 42-8.

23. L. Habachi, *Tell Basta*, Supplément aux Annales du Service des Antiquités de l'Égypte, no. 22, Cairo (1957), pp. 97-102.

24. D. Downes, *The Excavations at Esna 1905-1906,* Warminster (1974) pp. 18-24.

25. See recently M. Fitzenreiter, in B. Arnst, I. Hafemann & A. Lohwasser (eds), *Begegnungen, Antike Kulturen im Niltal*, Leipzig (2001), pp. 131-59.

26. For good colour photographs see Egyptian Antiquities Organization, *El Kab* (no date and no place of publication).

27. J. Malek, *SAK* 12 (1985), pp. 44-60.

28. *PM* I(2), 2nd ed., pp. 773-4, pl. XVI.

29. *Mummies & Magic*, p. 159, no. 110.

30. M. Raven, *The Tomb of Iurudef, A Memphite Official in the Reign of Ramesses II*, London (1991).

31. H. Schäfer, *Priestergräber und andere Grabfunde vom Ende des Alten Reiches bis zur griechischen Zeit vom Totentempel des Ni-user-rê*, Leipzig (1908), pp. 113-14, pl. 1.

8. The Third Intermediate Period:
The Peak of Coffin Production

1. The papyri are discussed by A. Niwinski, *Studies on the Illustrated Theban Funerary Papyri of the 11th and 10th Centuries BC*, Orbis Biblicus et Orientalis 86, Freiburg/Göttingen (1989); compare in general A. Niwinski, *21st Dynasty Coffins from Thebes, Chronological and Typological Studies*, Theben 5, Mainz (1988).

2. M. Raven, *OMRO* 59-60 (1978-79) pp. 251-96.

3. N. Reeves, *Valley of the Kings: The Decline of a Royal Necropolis*, London/New York (1990), pp. 277-8; K. Jansen-Winkeln, *ZÄS* 122 (1995), pp. 62-78.

4. Recent summaries: Reeves, op. cit. in n. 3, pp. 183-92; K. Jansen-Winkeln in *Deir el-Medina in the Third Millennium AD*, edited by R.J. Demarée & A. Egberts, Leiden (2000), pp. 163-70.

5. *Mummies & Magic*, pp. 162-3 (n. 115). The whole tomb was still being used in later times and finally became a mass burial. For a discussion of these Osiris-figures see: D. Aston, *JEA* 77 (1991) pp. 95-107.

6. This is a common burial place for kings, members of the royal family and high officials in the Third Intermediate Period and Late Period; J. Spencer, *Excavations* at *Tell el-Balamun 1995-1998*, London (1999), pp. 70-2; D. Aston, *Egyptian Pottery of the Late New Kingdom and the Third Intermediate Period (Twelfth-Seventh Century BC)*, SAGA 13, Heidelberg (1996), p. 40.

7. P. Montet, *La nécropole royale de Tanis II: Les constructions et le tombeau de Psousennès à Tanis*, Paris (1951), pp. 69-89.

8. *Mummies & Magic*, pp. 166-8.

9. A summary on the later tombs in the Ramesseum: F. Hassanein, G. Lecuyot, A.M. Loyrette & M. Nelson, *Studien zur Altägyptischen Kultur, Beihefte 2*, Akten des Vierten Internationalen Ägyptologischen Kongresses München 1985, edited by S. Schoske, Hamburg (1991), 181-97; compare H. Guichard & M. Kalos, *Memnonia* 11 (2000), pp. 47-69. The Abydos chapels: D. Randall-Maciver & A.C. Mace, *El-Amrah and Abydos 1899-1901*, EEF XXIII. London (1902), pp. 77-81, pls XXV-XXVIII.

10. Other tombs in a temple where found at Tell Moqdam, H. Gauthier, *ASAE* 21 (1921), pp. 21-7.

11. A. Badawi, *ASAE* 54 (1957) pp. 153-77; the nearby tomb of Petiese contained a re-used sarcophagus of the Nineteenth Dynasty and a silver coffin, Badawi, *ASAE* 44 (1944), pp. 181-2, pl. XXI.

12. M.F. Mostafa, *Das Grab des Neferhotep und des Meh (TT 257)*, Theben 8. Mainz am Rhein (1995), pp. 79-80, no. 84; example from Saqqara: S. Hassan, *Mastabas of Ny-'ankh-Pepy and Others* (General Organisation for Government Printing Offices Cairo 1975) pp. 80-3, 103, pls LV-LX, LXII, LXXXII.

13. J.E. Quibell, *The Ramesseum, The Tomb of Ptah-hotep*, BSAE II, London (1898), pp. 10-11.

14. H. Carter, *ASAE* 2 (1901), pp. 144-5; A good colour photograph of the coffin can be seen in N. Reeves & J. Taylor, *Howard Carter before Tutankhamun*, London (1992), p. 69.

15. Earl of Carnavon & H. Carter, *Five Years' Explorations at Thebes*, London/New York/Toronto/Melbourne (1912), pp. 24-6; for the dating: Reeves & Taylor, op. cit., p. 90.

16. G. Brunton, *Matmar*, London (1948), pls LIV-LVI (tomb register). Discussion of the date: Aston, *Cahiers Céramique Égyptienne* 4 (1996), pp. 35-6

9. The Late Period and Persian Domination

1. Recently discussed in E. Graefe, *Sat-Sobek und Peti-Imen-menu*. Hamm (2001), pp. 23-42.

2. W.M.F. Petrie & E. Mackay, *Heliopolis, Kafr Ammar and Shurafa*, BSAE 24, London (1915), p. 33; for the dating of these tombs: D. Aston, *Egyptian Pottery of the Late New Kingdom and the Third Intermediate Period (Twelfth-Seventh Century BC)*. SAGA 13, Heidelberg (1996), p. 36.

3. The burial of Tadja is not yet fully published; for a summary with some good pictures see R. Germer, *Das Geheimnis der Mumien, Ewiges Leben am Nil*, 2nd ed., München/New York (1998), pp. 144-5; some objects are published in photographs or are at least mentioned in W. Kaiser, *Ägyptisches Museum Berlin*, Berlin 1967, nos 613 (erroneously described there as from Thebes), 698, 701, 951 and in S. Schoske, B. Kreißl & R. Gremer, *'Anch' Blumen für das Leben*, Schriften aus der ägyptischen Sammlung 6, München (1992), nos 104, 133, 137, 157.

4. W.M. F. Petrie, G. Brunton & M. Murray, *Lahun II*, BSAE 33, London (1923), p. 36, pl. XLVIII (tomb register) for the dating: D. Aston, *Egyptian Pottery of the Late New Kingdom and the Third Intermediate Period (Twelfth-Seventh Century BC)*, SAGA 13, Heidelberg (1996), pp. 37-9; for other contemporary tombs with pottery and some few daily life objects see W.M.F. Petrie & E. Mackay, *Heliopolis, Kafr Ammar and Shurafa*, BSAE 24, London (1915), p. 35.

5. Fully published examples: U. Verhoeven, *Das Saitische Totenbuch der Iahetsnacht P.Colon.Aeg. 10207.* Payrologische Texte und Abhandlungen 41, Bonn (1993); U. Verhoeven, *Das Totenbuch des Monthpriesters Nespasefy aus der Zeit Psammetichs I*, Handschriften des Altaegyptischen Totenbuches 5, Wiesbaden (1999).

6. M.-L. Buhl, *The Late Egyptian Anthropoid Stone Sarcophagi*, Copenhagen (1959), pp. 178-9.

7. A. Awadalla & S. El-Sawy, *BIFAO* 90 (1990), pp. 29-39.

8. W. Seipel, *Ägypten, Götter, Gräber und die Kunst, 4000 Jahre Jenseitsglaube*, Linz (1989), p. 158, no. 124.

9. H. Gauthier, *ASAE* 33 (1933), pp. 27-53; a summary of the cemetery of Heliopolis at that time: S. Bickel & P. Tallet, *BIFAO* 97 (1997), pp. 67-90. Similar monuments were found in all parts of the country (just a few examples): H. Abou Seif, *ASAE* 26 (1926), pp. 32-43.

10. W.M.F. Petrie, *Gizeh and Rifeh*, BSAE XIII, London (1907), pp. 28-29, pls XXXII-XXXVII; W. el-Sadek, *Twenty-Sixth Dynasty Necropolis at Gizeh*, Vienna (1984).

11. Tomb of Nes-Thot (reign of Psamtek I), PM 2,2 (III), pp. 669-70.

12. L. Bareš, *Abusir IV, The Shaft Tomb of Udjahorresnet at Abusir*, Prague (1999) pp. 26-27, n. 50.

13. A. Barsanti, *ASAE* 5 (1904), pp. 69-78; G. Maspero, *ASAE* 5 (1904), pp. 78-83.

14. The tomb has been republished in E. Bresciani, S. Pernigotti & M.P. Giangeri Silvis, *La tomba di Ciennehebu, capo dell flota del re*, Pisa (1977).

15. M. Basta, *ASAE* 59 (1966), pp. 15-22, especially 20-1.

16. M. Chaban, *ASAE* 17 (1917), pp. 177-82.

17. H.D. Schneider, *JEA* 77 (1991), pp. 12-13.

18. I. Mathieson, *JEA* 81 (1995), pp. 23-41.

19. G. Jéquier, *Deux pyramides du moyen empire*, Fouilles à Saqqarah, Cairo (1933), pp. 49-52, pls XI-XII.

20. D. Arnold, in C. Berger & B. Mathieu (eds), *Études sur l'Ancien Empire et la nécropole de Saqqâra, dédiés à Jean-Philippe Lauer*, Orientalia Monspeliensia IX, Montpellier (1997), pp. 31-54; similar tombs were found in other parts of the country; see for example M. Sabottka, *ASAE* 69 (1983), pp. 147-51.

21. E. Bresciani, S. el-Naggar, S. Pernigotti & F. Silvano, *Galleria di Padineit, Visir di Nectanebi I, Saqqara I, Tomba di Boccori*, Pisa (1983).

22. M. Bietak & E. Reiser-Haslauer, *Das Grab des Anch-Hor II*, Wien (1982), pp. 183-224, 285-9.

23. W.M.F. Petrie, *Abydos I. 1902*, EEF 22, London (1902), pp. 37-8, pl. LXXVI-LXXIX, 1-5; LXXX (G 50).

24. L. Giddy, *The Anubieion at Saqqara II: The Cemeteries*, with a preface and contributions by H.S. Smith and an chapter by P.G. French, EES 56, London (1992); Similar burials are also known from other areas at Saqqara and Abusir: J.E. Quibell & A.G.K. Hayter, *Teti Pyramid North Side*, Cairo (1927), pls 1, 6; E. Strouhal & L. Bareš, *Secondary Cemetery in the Mastaba of Ptahshepses at Abusir*, Prague (1993); F. Janot, C. Bridonneau, M.-Fr. de Rozières, L. Cotelle-Michel & C. Decamps, *BIFAO* 101 (2001), pp. 249-91.

25. H. Schäfer, *Priestergräber und andere Grabfunde vom Ende des Alten Reiches bis zur griechischen Zeit vom Totentempel des Ni-user-re*, Leipzig (1908), pp. 122-4 (Sp 14).

10. Ptolemaic Egypt:
The Hellenistic World and Egyptian Beliefs

1. The Ptolemaic and Roman levels, even at cemeteries, are always the top levels. These were therefore the first tombs opened when travellers interested in buying Egyptian antiquities arrived in Egypt in the nineteenth century.

2. J. Taylor in: S. Walker & M.L. Bierbrier, *Ancient Faces: Mummy Portraits from Roman Egypt*, London (1997), pp. 34-35; M. Pohl, in B. Arnst, I. Hafemann & A. Lohwasser (eds), *Begegnungen, Antike Kulturen im Niltal*, Leipzig (2001), pp. 407-8, figs 1-5; Kischkewitz, in: *Ägyptisches Museum Berlin*, Edited by K.-H. Priese, Mainz (1991), pp. 214-15, no. 131. The exact datings of these pieces is not known, they are perhaps already early Roman.

3. W.M. F. Petrie & E. Mackay, *Heliopolis, Kafr Ammar and Shurafa*, BSAE 24, London (1915), p. 38, pls XLI-XLIV.

4. A. Abdalla, *Graeco-Roman Funerary Stelae from Upper Egypt*, Liverpool (1992), p. 5, pl. 76.

5. S. Walker & M.L. Bierbrier, *Ancient Faces: Mummy Portraits from Roman Egypt,* London (1997), pp. 29-30.

6. H. Schäfer, *Priestergräber und andere Grabfunde vom Ende des Alten Reiches bis zur griechischen Zeit vom Totentempel des Ni-user-re*, Leipzig (1908), pp. 119-22 (Sp 12).

7. H. Steckeweh, *Die Fürstengräber von Qâw*, Veröffentlichungen der Ernst von Sieglin-Expedition in Ägypten 6, Leipzig (1936), pp. 55-72.

8. The publication gives only a photograph, which is not clear.

9. C.M. Firth, *The Archaeological Survey of Nubia, Report for 1908-1909,* 2 vols, Cairo (1912), I, pp. 30-4; II, pls 22-31 (cemetery 89).

11. Egypt in the Roman Empire

1. S. Walker & M.L. Bierbrier, *Ancient Faces: Mummy Portraits from Roman Egypt,* London (1997), pp. 84-5, no. 74.

2. Walker & Bierbrier, op. cit., pp. 77-9, nos 54-6; R. Germer, *Das Geheimnis der Mumien, Ewiges Leben am Nil*, 2nd ed., München, New York (1998), pp. 146-7, figs 151, 152; S. Ikram & A. Dodson, *The Mummy in Ancient Egypt*, London (1998), p. 188, figs 220-1.

3. B. Borg, '*Der zierlichste Anblick der Welt ...*' Ägyptische Porträtmumien, Sonderhefte der Antike Welt, Mainz (1998), pp. 19-20.

4. Walker & Bierbrier, op. cit., pp. 30-6; O. Rubensohn & Knatz, *ZÄS* 41 (1904), pp. 10-13, figs 8, 10, 11.

5. Walker & Bierbrier. op. cit., p. 36, no. 10; H. Kischkewitz in *Ägyptisches Museum Berlin*, edited by K.-H. Priese, Mainz (1991), pp. 214-15, no. 131.

6. Late 'semi'-anthropoid example: C. Riggs, *JEA* 86 (2000), p. 136, pl. XVIII, 1: 'early second century'; a similar coffin: E. Brunner-Traut & H. Brunner, *Die Ägyptische Sammlung der Universität Tübingen*, Mainz (1981), pp. 234-3, pls 156-7 (said to come from Memphis).

7. D. Kurth, *Der Sarg der Teüris*, Mainz (1990).

8. S. Quirke in W.V. Davies (ed.), *Studies in Egyptian Antiquities: A Tribute to T.G.H. James.* British Museum Occasional Paper no. 123, London (1999), pp. 83-98; M. Coenen, *JEA* 86 (2000), pp. 81-98.

9. Quirke in Davies (ed.), op. cit., pp. 83-98; Coenen, op. cit., pp. 81-98.

10. W.M.F. Petrie & E. Mackay, *Heliopolis, Kafr Ammar and Shurafa*, BSAE 24, London (1915), p. 38.

11. S. Farid, *ASAE* 61 (1973), p. 25; A. Hamada & S. Farid, *ASAE* 48 (1948), p. 330 gives a list of coins found at Kom el-Karaz (East Delta), they date from Cleopatra VII to Marcus Aurelius. The list is ambiguous since not all coins were found in clear context next to a mummy. At Abou Billou they range from Cleopatra VII to Constantine I (A. Abdalla, *Graeco-Roman Funerary Stelae from Upper Egypt*, 7; S. El-Nassery & G. Wagner, *BIFAO* 78 (1978), p. 234); coins from burials of the Ptolemaic period: *Mummies & Magic*, pp. 195-6, no. 142.

12. W.M.F. Petrie & E. Mackay, *Heliopolis, Kafr Ammar and Shurafa*, p. 38 (tomb 99). The evidence is uncertain. Perhaps the woman was mummified, but nothing survived from the linen; however, the conditions for preservation of organic material in Kafr Ammar are good. A mummification would surely have been mentioned in the publication.)

13. A. Abdalla, *Graeco-Roman Funerary Stelae from Upper Egypt*, Liverpool (1992).

14. W.M.F. Petrie, *Dendereh 1898*, EE 17, London (1900), pls XXVIA-B; translations in G. Vittmann, *ZÄS* 112 (1985), pp. 153-68.

15. Petrie, op. cit., pp. 31-3.

16. J.E. Quibell & A.G.K. Hayter, *Teti Pyramid North Side: Excavations at Saqqara*, Cairo (1927), pl. 3.

17. E. Castel & F. Dunand, *BIFAO* 81 (1981), pp. 77-110.

18. The burial of Padiimenipet is now fully described in F.R. Herbin, *Padiimenipet fils de Sôter*, Paris (2002).

19. C. Riggs, *JEA* 86 (2000), pp. 121-44.

Chronology

This list includes only dynasties and kings mentioned in the text.

c. 5200-4000 BC	Fayum Neolithic
c. 4800-4200 BC	Merimde
c. 4600-4400 BC	Omari
c. 4400-4000 BC	Badari
c. 4000-3500 BC	Maadi-Buto
c. 4000-3500 BC	Naqada I
c. 3500-3200 BC	Naqada II
c. 3200-3000 BC	Naqada III
c. 3000-2700 BC	Early Dynastic Period
c. 2700-2200 BC	Old Kingdom
	Third Dynasty
	Djoser
	Fourth Dynasty
	Snefru
	Khufu
	Fifth Dynasty
	Djedkare Isesi
	Unas
	Sixth Dynasty
	Pepy I
	Pepy II
c. 2200-2050 BC	First Intermediate Period
	Eighth Dynasty
	Ibi
c. 2050-1650 BC	Middle Kingdom
	Eleventh Dynasty
	Mentuhotep II
	Twelfth Dynasty
	Amenemhat I
	Senusret I
	Senusret II
	Senusret III
	Amenemhat III
	Amenemhat IV
	Thirteenth Dynasty
	Hor
c. 1650-1550 BC	Second Intermediate Period
	Fifteenth Dynasty (Hyksos Period)
	Seventeenth Dynasty
	Djehuty
	Antef Nubkheperre

147

c. 1550-1070 BC	New Kingdom
	Eighteenth Dynasty
	Hatshepsut
	Thutmosis III
	Amenhotep II
	Thutmosis IV
	Amenhotep III
	Akhnaton
	Tutankhamun
	Eje
	Nineteenth Dynasty
	Sety I
	Ramses II
	Twentieth Dynasty
	Ramses III
	Ramses VI
	Ramses XI
c. 1070-664 BC	Third Intermediate Period
	Twenty-First Dynasty
	Psusennes
	Twenty-Second Dynasty
	Sheshonq I
	Osorkon I
	Osorkon II
664-525 BC	Late Period
	Twenty-Sixth Dynasty
	Psamtek I
	Apries
	Twenty-Seventh Dynasty (Persian Domination)
	Thirtieth Dynasty
	Nectanebo I
	Thirty-First Dynasty (Second Persian Domination)
310-30 BC	Ptolemaic Period
	Ptolemy III
30 BC – AD 395	Roman Period

Glossary

Amduat: 'What is in the Underworld' – text and images describing the journey of the sun-god Ra through the underworld each night. In the New Kingdom the composition is found mainly on the walls of kings' tombs. In the Third Intermediate Period it is often written on papyrus and placed in elite tombs. In the Late Period the text also appears on sarcophagi.

ankh-sign: hieroglyphic sign and amulet meaning 'life'.

atef-crown: crown with two feathers, often worn by Osiris.

ba-bird: a bird with a human head, representing one aspect of the human soul, especially after death. The ba was able to fly freely to and from the body.

benu-bird: sacred bird (heron) of the sun god Ra, symbolising rebirth.

Bes: god in the shape of a lion-faced dwarf. He offered protection at childbirth and is therefore often depicted on monuments connected with mother and child.

'Book of Breathing': Egyptian title of a funerary composition of the late Ptolemaic and Roman period.

'Book of the Dead': modern name for a group of about two hundred funerary texts, known in Egyptian as the 'Formulae for Going Out by Day'. Selections are found in elite burials from the mid-Eighteenth Dynasty to Ptolemaic times, and in New Kingdom kings' tombs. The best known copies are on papyri buried with the dead person. The single chapters have been numbered by modern scholars.

button seal: small round seal, in common use in the First Intermediate Period.

canopic box: box for the entrails, or the vases containing the entrails (**canopic jars**).

cartonnage: layers of gummed linen and plaster, most often put together to form mummy masks and mummy cases. In the Ptolemaic period scrap paper was used instead of linen. The word cartonnage is also used to refer to whole body mummy cases made out of the material.

djed-pillar: hieroglyphic sign amulet meaning 'duration'.

false door: essential part of Old Kingdom mastaba decoration. On the false door the tomb-owner is shown sitting in front of an offering table receiving food for the afterlife. The false door was also the place from which the ba (see above) of the dead person could leave the tomb.

heart scarab: scarab bearing the text of 'Book of the Dead' spell 30, placed on the mummy's chest. Heart scarabs appear for the first time at the end of the Middle Kingdom and are quite common in the New Kingdom. They were used until the Ptolemaic period.

Horus: god of kingship, son of Isis and Osiris.

Isis: goddess, wife of Osiris.

ka: in Egyptian religion, the essential part of the human being, roughly translated by 'soul' or 'spirit'. While the body in tombs could decay, the ka lived on and could occupy statues.

kohl: Arabic for galena (a lead ore), commonly used for eye-paint. Cosmetic vessels in which it was kept are called **kohl pots**.

Libya: neighbour of Ancient Egypt to the west. Ancient Egyptian kings were often at war with Libya. Most rulers of the Third Intermediate and Late Period are of Libyan origin.

magical bricks: four bricks inscribed with a special spell and placed in many New Kingdom and Late Period elite tombs.

mastaba: mud or stone building, often almost solid, on top of a burial chamber. Mastabas of people of high status are often decorated with reliefs and statues. Smaller mastabas can be quite small and simple.

mummy board: mummy-shaped board placed on many mummies from the Nineteenth to the early Twenty-Second Dynasty.

mummy mask: mask placed over the head of the mummy. Mummy masks appear first at the end of the Old Kingdom and are very popular in the First Intermediate Period and Middle Kingdom. In the New Kingdom and Late Period they appear sporadically, while they are again very popular in Ptolemaic and Roman times.

natron: naturally occurring cleaning agent, a compound of sodium salts. Used to dry the body in mummification.

Nubia: neighbour of Ancient Egypt to the south.

Nut: goddess of the sky.

offering list: written list on stelae, in tomb chapels, on coffins and other places, naming important items for the underworld. Written words replace the objects, principally items of food and drink.

opening of the mouth: ritual performed with statues and mummies to bring them to life.

Osiris: god of the underworld.

palace façade: the mastabas of elite tombs belonging mainly to the First Dynasty are decorated with a brick-built niche structure, assumed to copy contemporary palace façades. A similar pattern is found as painted (and sometimes relief) decoration on coffin and sarcophagi of the Old and Middle Kingdom

sarcophagus: coffin made of stone. The first box-shaped examples appear under Djoser. Sarcophagi are very common in the Old and Middle Kingdom for highest elite burials. In the Eighteenth Dynasty, with few exceptions, they are attested only for royal burials, but become quite common in the Nineteenth Dynasty. The New Kingdom private examples are mostly anthropoid, while the royal sarcophagi are box-shaped. Sarcophagi became common again in the Late Period and Ptolemaic times.

sed-festival: principal festival of kingship.

serdab: room for statues in the overground part (mastaba) of Old Kingdom tombs. Serdabs are not common after that time.

seven sacred oils: essential part of elite burials in the Old and Middle Kingdom. They are either placed in seven vessels in the burial or named in the tomb decoration, on the coffin or in the offering list.

shabti-figures: small – often mummy-shaped – figures. A special spell on the figures expresses their function, namely, to carry out heavy manual tasks on behalf of a person in the afterlife.

Sokar bark: the bark of Sokar, god of the cemetery of Memphis (Saqqara).

solar boat: the boat in which the sun god Ra travels across the sky by day and the underworld by night.

tiyet: amulet, also often called 'blood of Isis'. Symbol of the goddess Isis, its original meaning is uncertain.

vignettes: small illustrations on coffins or in papyri.

wedjat-eye: the eye of Horus, which plays an important role in Egyptian mythology. Wedjat-eyes are very common amulets.

Further Reading

Abbreviations follow the *Lexikon der Ägyptologie*, Wiesbaden.

General

Sue D'Auria, P. Lacovara & C.H. Roehrig (eds), *Mummies & Magic: The Funerary Arts of Ancient Egypt*, (1988)
W. Forman & S. Quirke, *Hieroglyphs and the Afterlife in Ancient Egypt*, London (1996)
S. Ikram & A.Dodson, *The Mummy in Ancient Egypt*, London (1998)
N. Kanawati, *The Tomb and Beyond: Burial Customs of Egyptian Officials*, Warminster (2001)
W. Seipel, *Ägypten: Götter, Gräber und die Kunst, 4000 Jahre Jenseitsglaube*, Linz (1989)
A. J. Spencer, *Death in Ancient Egypt*, Harmondsworth (1982)
Taylor, J.H., *Death and the Afterlife in Ancient Egypt*, London (2001)
See also Digital Egypt for Universities on the web:
http://www.petrie.ucl.ac.uk/digital_egypt/Welcome.html

Burial customs in specific periods

J. Bourriau, 'Patterns of change in burial customs', in S. Quirke (ed), *Middle Kingdom Studies*, New Malden (1991), pp. 3-20
J.-L. Podwin. 'Position du mobilier funéraire dans les tombes égyptiens privées du Moyen Empire', *MDAIK* 56 (2000), pp. 277-334
S.J. Seidlmayer, *Gräberfelder aus dem Übergang vom Alten zum Mittleren Reich*, Studien zur Archäologie und Geschichte Altägyptens 1, Heidelberg (1990)
St. T. Smith, 'Intact tombs of the Seventeenth and Eighteenth Dynasties from Thebes and the New Kingdom burial system', *MDAIK* 48 (1992), pp. 193-231

The 'Book of the Dead' and funerary papyri

T.G. Allen, *The Book of the Dead or Going Forth by Day*, Chicago (1974)
I. Munro, *Untersuchungen zu den Totenbuch-Papyri der 18. Dynastie. Kriterien ihrer Datierung*, Studies in Egyptology, London/New York (1988)
I. Munro, *Die Totenbuch-Handschriften der 18. Dynastie im Ägyptischen Museum Cairo*, Wiesbaden (1994)
E. Naville, *Das Ägyptische Totenbuch der XVIII. bis XX. Dynastie 1*, Berlin (1886)
A. Niwinski, *Studies on the Illustrated Theban Funerary Papyri of the 11th and 10th Centuries BC*, Orbis Biblicus et Orientalis 86, Göttingen (1989)

Coffins

M. Barwik, 'Typology and dating of the "white" type anthropoid coffins of the early XVIIIth Dynasty', *Études et Travaux* XVIII (1999), pp. 8-33
M.-L. Buhl, *The Late Egyptian Anthropoid Stone Sarcophagi*, Copenhagen (1959)

Further Reading

G. Lapp, *Typologie der Särge und Sargkammern von der 6. bis 13. Dynastie*, Studien zur Archäologie und Geschichte Altägyptens 7, Heidelberg (1994)

A. Niwinski, *21st Dynasty Coffins from Thebes, Chronological and Typological Studies*, Theben 5, Mainz (1988)

A.M. Donadoni Roveri, *I Sarcofagi Egizi dalle Origini alla Fine dell' Antico Regno*, Rome (1969)

J.H. Taylor, *Egyptian Coffins*, London (1989)

J.H. Taylor, 'Patterns of colouring on ancient Egyptian coffins from the New Kingdom to the Twenty-Sixth Dynasty: an overview', in *Colour and Painting in Ancient Egypt*, edited by W.V. Davies, London (2001), pp. 164-81

R. van Walsem, *The Coffin of Djedmonthuiufankh in the National Museum of Antiquities at Leiden: Technical and Iconographic/Iconographical Aspects*, Leiden (1997)

H. Willems, *Chests of Life*, Leiden (1988)

H. Willems, *The Coffin of Heqata*, Orientalia Lovaniensia Analecta 70, Leuven (1996)

Canopic jars and chests

D.A. Aston, 'Canopic chests from the Twenty-First Dynasty to the Ptolemaic Period', *Ägypten und Levante* X (2000), pp. 159-78

A. Dodson, *The Canopic Equipment of the Kings of Egypt*, London and New York (1994)

B. Lüscher, *Untersuchungen zu ägyptischen Kanopenkästen*, Hildesheimer Ägyptologische Beiträge 31, Hildesheim (1990)

V. Raisman & G.T. Martin, *Canopic Equipment in the Petrie Collection*, Warminster (1984)

Shabtis and shabti boxes

D.A. Aston, 'The shabti box: a typological study', *OMRO* 74 (1994), pp. 21-54

L. Aubert, *Les statuettes funéraires de la Deuxième Cachette à Deir el-Bahari*. Paris (1998)

G.T. Martin, 'Shabtis of private persons in the Amarna period', *MDAIK* 42 (1986), pp. 109-29

F. Poole, 'Social implications of the shabti custom in the New Kingdom', in *Egyptological Studies for Claudio Barocas*, edited by Rosanna Pirelli, Naples (1999), pp. 95-113

H.D. Schneider, *Shabtis I-III*, Leiden (1977)

H.M. Stewart, *Egyptian Shabtis*, Princes Risborough (1995)

Figures in Late Period tombs

D.A. Aston, 'Two Osiris figures of the Third Intermediate Period', *JEA* 77 (1991), pp. 95-107

M.J. Raven, 'Papyrus sheaths and Ptah-Sokar-Osiris statues', *OMRO* 59-60 (1978-9), pp. 251-96

Corn mummies ('Osiris bed')

M.J. Raven, 'Corn mummies', *OMRO* 63 (1982), pp. 7-38

Further Reading

The 'opening of the mouth' ceremony

E. Otto, *Das ägyptische Mundöffnungsritual*, Wiesbaden (1960)

A.M. Roth., 'Fingers, stars, and the 'opening of the mouth': the nature and function of the NTRWJ-blades', *JEA* 79 (1993), pp. 57-79

R. van Walsem, 'The psš-kf: an investigation of an Ancient Egyptian funerary instrument', *OMRO* 59 (1978-9), pp. 193-249

Hypocephali

E. Varga, 'Les travaux préliminaires de la monographie sur les hypocephales', *Acta Orientalia* XII (1961), pp. 235-47

Inscribed mummy bandages

A. De Caluwe, *Un 'Livre des Morts' sur bandelette de momie*, Bruxelles (1991)

Roman Egypt

B. Borg, *Mumienporträts: Chronologie und kultureller Kontext*, Mainz (1996)

E. Doxiadis, *The Mysterious Fayum Portraits: Faces from Ancient Egypt*, Singapore (1994)

G. Grimm, *Die römischen Mumienmasken aus Ägypten*, Wiesbaden (1974)

K. Parlasca, *Mumienporträts und verwandte Denkmäler*, Wiesbaden (1966)

K. Parlasca, H. Seemann (editors), *Augenblicke: Mumienporträts und ägyptische Grabkunst aus römischer Zeit*, Munich (1999)

S. Walker & M.L. Bierbrier, *Ancient Faces: Mummy Portraits from Roman Egypt*, London (1997)

Figure Sources

Fig. 1: Wolfram Grajetzki.

Fig. 2: Wolfram Grajetzki.

Fig. 3: after F. Debono & B. Mortinson, *El Omari*, Archäologische Veröffentlichungen 82, Mainz (1990), pl. 4.6-9.

Fig. 4: after I. Rizkana & J. Seeher, *Maadi IV: The Predynastic Cemeteries of Maadi and Wadi Digla*, Archäologische Veröffentlichungen 81, Mainz (1990), p. 58.

Fig. 5: after G. Brunton & G. Caton-Thompson, *The Badarian Civilisation*, BSAE 46. London (1928) pls VII, IX.

Fig. 6: after G. Dreyer et al., *MDAIK* 52 (1996), pp. 25-6, fig. 3.

Fig. 7: after R. Engelbach, *Harageh*, BSAE 28, London (1923), pp. 13-14, pl. XIII.

Fig. 8: J. de Morgan, *Recherches sur les origines de l'Égypte: ethnographie préhistorique et tombeau royal de Négadah*, Paris (1897), fig. 521.

Fig. 9: de Morgan, op. cit., fig. 515.

Fig. 10: de Morgan, op. cit., figs 685, 686.

Fig. 11: after W.E. Emery, *Great Tombs of the first Dynasty II*, EES 46, London (1954), p. 141.

Fig. 12: after Emery, op. cit., p. 26.

Fig. 13: after A.J. Spencer, *Catalogue of Egyptian Antiquities in the British Museum V. Early Dynastic Objects*. London (1980), pl. 7.

Fig. 14: A. Mariette, *Les Mastabas de l'Ancien Empire*, Paris (1889), p. 80.

Fig. 15: after *PM* III.I (2), XVII-XXXIX.

Fig. 16: J.E. Quibell, R.F.E. Paget, A.A. Pirie & F.Ll. Griffith, *The Ramesseum, The Tomb of Ptah-hetep*, London (1898), pls XXXI-XLI

Fig. 17: after H. Junker, *Giza I. Die Mastabas der IV. Dynastie auf dem Westfriedhof*, Wien/Leipzig (1929), pl. XIId.

Fig. 18: after Junker, op. cit., p. 55.

Fig. 19: after D. Arnold (ed.), *Egyptian Art in the Age of Pyramids*, New York (1999), pp. 387-8, no. 136; p. 390, no. 138.

Fig. 20: after H. Kammerer-Grothaus in B. Ginter, J.K. Kozlowski, M. Pawlilowski, J. Sliwa & H. Kammerer-Grothaus, *Frühe Keramik und Kleinfunde aus El-Tarif*, Archäologische Veröffentlichungen 40, Mainz (1998), pp. 67-9.

Fig. 21: after S. Hassan, *Excvations at Giza III (1931-1932)*, Cairo (1941), pp. 78-92.

Fig. 22: after Hassan, op. cit., pp. 13-47.

Figs 23-5: after H. Junker, *Giza VII. Der Ostabschnitt des Westfriedhofs I*, Wien/Leipzig (1944), pp. 48-61.

Fig. 26: after Junker, op. cit. (for good colour photographs see W. Seipel (ed.), *Gold der Pharaonen*, Vienna (2001), pp. 33-7, nos 18-20).

Fig. 27: after G.A. Reisner, *A Provincial Cemetery of the Pyramid Age: Naga ed-Dêr III*, Oxford (1932), 242.

Fig. 28: after K.R. Weeks, *Mastabas of Cemetery G 6000*, Giza Mastabas 5, Boston (1994), p. 89, fig. 116.

Figure Sources

Fig. 29: after G. Brunton & R. Engelbach, *Gurob*, BSAE 41 London (1927), pl. VII.15.

Fig. 30: *(left)* after Reisner, op. cit., 324-5; *(right)* after Brunton & Englebach, op. cit., pl. IV.

Fig. 31: after Reisner, op. cit., 331-2.

Fig. 32: after G. Jéquier, *Tombeaux de particuliers contemporains de Pepi II*, Fouilles à Saqqarah, Cairo (1929), p. 29, fig. 29.

Fig. 33: after A. el-Sawi, *Excavations at Tell Basta*, Prague (1979), fig. 148, 151.

Figs 34-6: after E. Naville, *The Cemeteries of Abydos I*. EES 33, London (1914) pp. 19-20, pl. IV, VI.

Fig. 37: after Naville, op. cit., p. 20, pl. IV, VI.

Figs 38-9: after M. Vallogia, *Le mastaba de Medou-nefer. Balat I*, FIFAO 31, Cairo (1986), pp. 84-93.

Fig. 40: after Vallogia, op. cit., pl. LXII

Fig. 41: G. Jéquier, *Tombeaux de particuliers contemporains de Pepi II*, Fouilles à Saqqarah, Cairo (1929), p. 19, fig. 17.

Fig. 42: Jéquier, op. cit., p. 25, fig. 23.

Fig. 43: after H. Junker, *Gîza VIII. Die Ostabschnitt des Westfriedhofs*, Wien (1947), 145, fig. 70.

Fig. 44: after Reisner, op. cit., 337.

Fig. 45. G. Steindorff, *Grabfunde des Mittleren Reiches in den königlichen Museen zu Berlin II, Der Sarg des Sebk-o – Einzelfunde aus Gebelen*, Berlin (1901), pl. III-IV.

Fig. 46: sketch after Photograph no. A 8281, Boston Museum of Fine Arts. Courtesy of the museum.

Fig. 47: after Brunton & Engelbach, op. cit., pl. XII.

Fig. 48: after G. Brunton, *Qau and Badari II*, BSAE 45 London (1928), pls LII, XLIV.

Fig. 49: after Brunton, op. cit., pls LXVI, XLVII.

Figs 50-4: after M. Jørgensen, *Catalogue Egypt I*, Copenhagen (1996), pp. 124-39, nos 48-55.

Fig. 55: after K. Sowada, T. Callaghan & P. Bentley, *The Teti Cemetery at Saqqara. IV: Minor Burials and Other Material*, Australian Centre for Egyptology, Reports 12,. Warminster (1999), pl. 4.

Fig. 56: J.-E. Gautier & G. Jéquier, *Mémoire sur les Fouilles de Licht*, Cairo (1902), pp. 97-9.

Fig. 57: reconstruction after J. de Morgan, *Fouilles à Dahchour. Mars-Juin 1894*, Vienne (1895), p. 28; L. Borchardt, *Denkmäler des Alten Reiches I. Catalogue Général des Antiquitiés Ègyptiennes du Musée du Cairo nos 1295-1808*, Berlin (1937), 158-64 (nos 1468-1477).

Fig. 58: after D. Arnold, *Egyptian Archaeology* 9 (1996), p. 39.

Fig. 59: after Ch. van Siclen, III, *BSAK* 4, p. 188, fig. 1.

Fig. 60 Gautier & Jéquier, op. cit., pl. XXVII.

Fig. 61: G. Daressy, *ASAE 1* (1900), p. 27, fig. 2.

Fig. 62: Daressy, op. cit., p. 32, fig. 1.

Fig. 63: Daressy, op. cit., p. 28, fig. 1.

Fig. 64: after D. Arnold, *Gräber des Alten und Mittleren Reiches in El-Tarif*, AV 17, Mainz (1976), p. 39, pl. 39, no. 8.

Fig. 65: after G. Brunton, *Qau and Badari III*, BSAE 50 London (1930), p. 1, pl. II.

Fig. 66: G. Kminek-Szedlo, *Saggio Filotogico per l'apprendimento della lingua e scrittura egizina Bologna e la interpretazione delle iscrizione geroglifiche che si leggono sui monumenti del Museo Civica di Bologna*, Bologna (1877), p. 33, pl. IX, fig. 3.

Figure Sources

Figs 67-9: J. de Morgan, *Fouilles a Dahchour. Mars-Juin 1894*, Vienne (1895), p. 91, fig. 211; 96, figs 221-5; 101, fig. 241; compare W. Grajetzki, *GM* 166 (1998) for the arrangement of the inscriptions.

Fig. 70: after Earl of Carnarvon & H. Carter, *Five Years' Explorations at Thebes*, London/New York/Toronto/Melbourne (1912), pp. 54-5.

Fig. 71: after R. Anthes, *MDAIK* 12 (1943) p. 6, figs. 2-3.

Fig. 72: after Anthes, op. cit., pp. 8-10, figs 5, 10.

Fig. 73: after M. Bietak, *Tell el-Da'a V, Ein Friedhofsbezirk der Mittleren Bronzezeitkultur mit Totentempel und Siedlungsschichten I*, Wien (1991), pp. 33-4.

Fig. 74: after Bietak, op. cit., pp. 51-60.

Fig. 75: after Bietak, op. cit., fig. 26.

Fig. 76: after Bietak, op. cit., fig. 26.

Fig. 77 (*left*): after Wainwright, *Balabish*, London (1920), pl. XV; (*right*) after Brunton, op. cit. above Fig. 65, p. 5, pls V, X.4.

Fig. 78: *Monuments divers recueilles en Ègypte et en Nubie*, texte par G. Maspero, Paris (1889), pl. 51.

Fig. 79: after C. Lilyquist in *Ancient Egypt, the Aegean, and the Near East: Studies in Honour of Martha Rhoads Bell*, edited by J. Phillips, San Antonio, Texas (1997), 312, fig. 3.

Fig. 80: after Lilyquist, op. cit., 323, fig. 11.

Fig. 81: after B. Engelmann-von Carnap, *Die Struktur des Thebanischen Beamtenfriedhofs in der ersten Hälfte der 18. Dynastie*, ADAIK 15 (1999), p. 70, fig. 48A (the plans are not oriented).

Figs 82-4: after W.M.F. Petrie, *Illahun, Kahun and Gurob*, London (1891), pl. XXVI-XXVII.

Fig. 85: after R. Engelbach, op. cit., pp. 13-14, pl. XIII.

Fig. 86: after Brunton, op. cit. above Fig. 65, p. 13, pl. XXII.

Fig. 87: after L. Loat, *Gurob*, together with M.A. Murray, *Saqqara Mastabas I*, BSAE X, London (1905), p. 2.

Figs 88-90: after T. Säve-Söderbergh & L. Troy, *New Kingdom Pharaonic Sites, The Finds and the Sites*, Scandinavian Joint Expedition 5: 2-3. Uppsala (1991), pl. 71.

Fig. 91: after Säve-Söderbergh & Troy, op. cit., pp. 171-2, pls 42:5, 43:4.

Fig. 92: after R. Holthoer, *New Kingdom Pharaonic Sites: The Pottery*, Scandinavian Joint Expedition 5:1, Uppsala (1977), passim.

Fig. 93: after W. Seipel, *Ägypten. Götter, Gräber und die Kunst, 4000 Jahre Jenseitsglaube*, Linz (1989), p. 207, no. 183.

Fig. 94: after B. Bruyère, *Rapport sur les fouilles de Deir el Médineh (1928)*, Cairo (1929), p. 37, fig. 24.

Fig. 95: after Bruyère, op. cit., pl. III (the coffin is published with a good colour photograph in G. Andreau (ed.), *Les artistes de Pharaon* (exhibition catalogue), Paris (2002), p. 303, no. 253; a good colour photograph of the painted textile can be found in *Parfums et cosmétiques dans l'Ègypte ancienne* (exhibition catalogue), Cairo/Paris/Marseille (2002), fig. on p. 115).

Fig. 96: after Bruyère, op. cit., pl. V

Fig. 97: after Bruyère, op. cit., p. 68, fig. 34, pls VII, VIII, X; *Les artistes de Pharaon*, p. 155, no. 100; 160-1, no. 108.

Fig. 98: after Bruyère, op. cit., p. 61, fig. 31, 67, fig. 33, 69, fig. 35.

Fig. 99: after Bruyère, op. cit., pl. VIII; *Les artistes de Pharaon*, p. 157, nos. 14a-b.

Fig. 100: after Bruyère, op. cit., pls X, XI; *Les artistes de Pharaon*, p. 292, no. 237.

Figs 101-6: after K. Sowada, T. Callaghan & P. Bentley, *The Teti Cemetery at*

Saqqara. IV: Minor Burials and Other Material, Australian Centre for Egyptology, Reports 12. Warminster (1999), p. 13 (94/3).

Fig. 107: R. Engelbach, *Riqqeh and Memphis VI*, BSAE 25, London (1915), pl. XXII; copyright Petrie Museum of Egyptian Archaeology, University College London.

Fig. 108: V. Schmidt, *Sarkofager, Levende og døde i det gamle Ægypten*, Copenhagen (1919), fig. 651.

Fig. 109: after E. Feucht, *Das Grab des Nefersecheru*, Theben II. Mainz (1985), pl. XLI, no. 122.

Fig. 110: after F. Kampp, *Die Thebanische Nekropole*, Theben 13 Mainz (1996), p. 237, fig. 134.

Fig. 111: after L. Habachi, *Tell Basta*, Supplément aux Annales du Service des Antiquités de l'Égypte, no. 22, Cairo (1957), fig. 27.

Fig. 112: after M. Raven, *The Tomb of Iurudef. A Memphite Official in the Reign of Ramesses II*, London (1991), pls 5, 10, 25, 26.

Fig. 113: after W. Seipel, *Ägypten: Götter, Gräber und die Kunst, 4000 Jahre Jenseitsglaube*, Linz (1989), p. 166, no. 132.

Fig. 114: Twenty-First Dynasty coffin, J.D. Guigniaut, *Description et essai d'explication des peintures symboliques et légendes hiéroglyphique d'une caisse de momie égyptienne conservée à Paris*, Paris (1825), p. 10.

Fig. 115: after M. Raven, *The Tomb of Maya and Meryt II, Ojects and Skeletal Remains*, EES Excavations Memoir 65, London (2001), p. 88.

Figs 116-25: sarcophagus and four canopic jars after P. Montet, *La nécropole royale de Tanis II: Les constructions et le tombeau de Psousennès à Tanis*, Paris (1951), pp. 69-89.

Fig. 126: after A. Badawi, *ASAE* 54 (1956-57), pl. XIVa, b.

Fig. 127: after Badawi, op. cit., pl. XVe.

Fig. 128: after Badawi, op. cit., pl. XIIIa.

Fig. 129: after W. Seipel, *Ägypten: Götter, Gräber und die Kunst, 4000 Jahre Jenseitsglaube*, Linz (1989), p. 342, no. 518.

Fig. 130: J.E. Quibell, *The Ramesseum, The Tomb of Ptah-hotep*, BSAE II, London (1898) pl. XVI, copyright University College London, Petrie Museum of Egyptian Archaeology.

Fig. 131 Quibell, op. cit., pls XVII, XVIII, copyright University College London, Petrie Museum of Egyptian Archaeology.

Fig. 132: after Earl of Carnavon & H. Carter, *Five Years' Explorations at Thebes*, London/New York/Toronto/Melbourne (1912), pl. XVII.2.

Fig. 133: G. Brunton, *Qau and Badari III*, BSAE 50, London (1930), pl. XLIV – the dwarf; copyright University College London, Petrie Museum of Egyptian Archaeology.

Fig. 134: after G. Brunton, *Matmar*, London (1948), pl. LXIII.

Fig. 135: after G. Brunton, op. cit., p. 75.

Fig. 136: after R. Anthes, *MDAIK* 12 (1943), pl. 4.

Fig. 137: after W.M.F. Petrie & E. Mackay, *Heliopolis, Kafr Ammar and Shurafa*, BSAE 24, London (1915), pl. XXXIV.

Fig. 138: after Petrie & Mackay, op. cit., pl. XXIX, 3, 4.

Fig. 139: after W.M.F. Petrie, G. Brunton & M. Murray, *Lahun II*, BSAE 33, London (1923), pl. L.

Fig. 140: H. von Minutoli, *Reise zum Tempel des Jupiter in der Libyschen Wüste und nach Ober-Aegypten in den Jahren 1820 und 1821*, 1-3, edited by Tölken, Berlin (1824-7), pl. 35, 1-2.

Fig. 141: after D. Eigner, *Die monumentalen Grabbauten der Spätzeit in der thebanischen Nekropole*, Vienna (1984), pp. 53-4.

Figure Sources

Fig. 142: after A. Barsanti, *ASAE* 5 (1904), p. 71, fig. 2; the shaft tomb of Tjanenehebu, Barsanti, *ASAE* 1 (1900), p. 263

Fig. 143: after E. Bresciani, S. Pernigotti & M.P. Giangeri Silvis, *La tomba di Ciennehebu, capo dell flota del re*, Pisa (1977), pl. XXX.

Fig. 144: after Bresciani, Pernigotti & Giangeri Silvis, op. cit., pl. LII.

Fig. 145: after Bresciani, Pernigotti & Giangeri Silvis, op. cit., pl. XLVIII.

Fig. 146: after Bresciani, Pernigotti & Giangeri Silvis, op. cit., pl. LXIII.

Fig. 147: after H. Schäfer, *Priestergräber und andere Grabfunde vom Ende des Alten Reiches bis zur griechischen Zeit vom Totentempel des Ni-user-re*, Leipzig (1908), p. 127

Fig. 148: after D. Arnold in C. Berger & B. Mathieu (editors), *Études sur l'Ancien Empire et la nécropole de Saqqara, dédiés à Jean-Philippe Lauer*, Orientalia Monspeliensia IX, Montpellier (1997), p. 44, fig. 6.

Fig. 149: A.E. Mariette, *Les mastabas de l'ancien empire*, Paris (1889), p. 555.

Fig. 150: Brunton, op. cit. above Fig 65, pl. XLIV.

Fig. 151: W. Pleyte, *Chapitres supplémentaires du Livre des Morts 162 à 174 I*, Leiden (1881), pl. between pp. 60 and 61.

Fig. 152: after L. Giddy, *The Anubieion at Saqqâra II: The Cemeteries*, with a preface and contributions by H.S. Smith and a chapter by P.G. French, EES 56, London (1992), pl. 44, 48, 75.

Fig. 153: after E. Breccia, *La necropoli di Sciatbi, Catalogue Général des Antiquités Égyptiennes (Musée d'Alexandrie)*, Cairo (1912), fig. 17.

Fig. 154: *Description de l'Égypte* A vol. II, pls 62-3.

Fig. 155: after B. Borg, *'Der zierlichste Anblick der Welt ...'*, Ägyptische Porträtmumien, Sonderhefte der Antike Welt, Mainz (1998), p. 19, fig. 21.

Fig. 156: F. Cailliaud, *Voyage à Méroé, au Fleuve Blanc, au-delà de Fâzoql dans le midi royaume de Sennâr, à Syouah et dans cinq autres oasis, fait dans les années 1819, 1820, 1821 et 1822*, vol. IV. Paris (1827), pl. LXVII.

Fig. 157: Cailliaud, op. cit., pl. LXX.

Fig. 158: after Riggs, *JEA* 86 (2000) fig. 1.

*

All drawings, if not otherwise stated, are by Wolfram Grajetzki.

Index

Index